MW01196342

CHINESE SUN

EX LIBRIS
ЦЫГАНКОВА

TRANSLATED BY EVGENY PAVLOV
EDITED BY TERRY MYERS

INTRODUCTION BY JACOB EDMOND

ARKADII DRAGOMOSHCHENKO

CHINESE SUN

UGLY DUCKLING PRESSE

EEPS IX   A·D·MMV

CHINESE SUN

Copyright 2005: Arkadii Dragomoshchenko;
Evgeny Pavlov; Jacob Edmond.

Originally published in Russian as *Kitaiskoe Solntse* by
Mitin Zhurnal and Borey Art Center, St. Petersburg, 1997.

Some parts of this translation have appeared in
BOMB Magazine, and *Crossing Centuries: the New Generations
in Russian Poetry* (Talisman House).

LIBRARY OF CONGRESS CATALOGING-IN-PUBLICATION DATA

Dragomoshchenko, A. (Arkadii)
 [Kitaiskoe solntse. English]
 Chinese sun / Arkadii Dragomoshchenko ; translated by Evgeny Pavlov ;
edited by Terry Myers ; introduction by Jacob Edmond.-- 1st ed.
  p. cm. -- (Eastern European poets series ; #9)
 ISBN-13: 978-1-933254-04-3 (pbk. : alk. paper)
 ISBN-10: 1-933254-04-1 (pbk. : alk. paper)
 I. Pavlov, Evgeny, 1968- II. Myers, Terry. III. Title. IV. Series.

PG3479.6.R28K5813 2005
891.71'44--dc22

        2005014406

First Edition | First Printing | 2005
Ugly Duckling Presse, 106 Ferris St., Brooklyn, NY
www.uglyducklingpresse.org

Distributed by SPD/Small Press Distribution
www.spdbooks.org

Cover design: Jeremy Mickel
Cover printing: Ugly Duckling Presse
Book Design: Don't Look Now!
Type: Chaparral and Trajan (by Carol Twombly); and Orator
Printing: McNaughton & Gunn, 50% post-consumer paper

CHINESE SUN

INTRODUCTION

Stein often begins literally with descriptions of things seen... Very quickly these become elements of description... By the time they are seen formally, as elements of composition, writing has begun.

—Ulla Dydo on Gertrude Stein

OVER THE PAST THIRTY YEARS, Arkadii Dragomoshchenko has consistently pushed the boundaries of Russian literature, deliberately positioning himself outside its "Great Tradition." His innovative approach to writing reflects not only his family origins outside the geographical boundaries of Russia but also his place within another tradition—the approach pioneered a century ago by Gertrude Stein and others in which language itself becomes the focus of the composition. *Chinese Sun* affirms once again Dragomoshchenko's vital place within this alternative tradition.

Born in Potsdam in 1946, Dragomoshchenko grew up in Vinnitsa, Ukraine. Moving to Leningrad in 1969, he quickly immersed himself in the burgeoning unofficial literary community of that city. He first came to prominence as a poet when his work was published in the unofficial Leningrad anthology *Lepta* (1975). Along with many other important writers of his generation, Drago-moshchenko worked outside official literary institutions prior to the perestroika period, winning accolades such as the inaugural Andrei Bely Prize in 1979, the first unofficial literary prize in the Soviet Union. He was unusual, however, because he rejected not just the official line but also traditional notions of literature, such as the concept of lyric "voice," which most unofficial poets accepted unquestioningly. While Dragomoshchenko could not help but be influenced by the intense mystical, religious, and philosophical approach common in Leningrad's unofficial literary community, he developed a more ironic, controversial style that drew on Russian avant-garde predecessors, such as the OBERIU writers Aleksandr Vvedensky and Konstantin Vaginov. In the 1980s, Dragomoshchenko became a leading representative of Russian literary postmodernism and today remains at the forefront of independent experimental literature, consistently producing innovative works in poetry, prose, and essay forms.

Since the mid-1980s, Dragomoshchenko has also had a presence in American literature, thanks in part to the efforts of his first American translator, the poet Lyn Hejinian. The two met in 1983, when Hejinian visited the Soviet Union for the first time, and quickly began corresponding and translating one another's work. Since that time, Dragomoshchenko's poetry has appeared widely in American poetry magazines and journals, and two books translated by Hejinian, *Description* (1990) and *Xenia* (1993), have also been published in the United States. In addition to translating each other's work, Dragomoshchenko and Hejinian have collaborated on a number of artistic projects, including the film *Letters Not about Love* (1998), which explores their intense personal and poetic relationship.

Published in Russian in 1997, *Chinese Sun* can be seen as developing out of two other ambitious works, *Xenia* and *Phosphor* (sadly, only extracts of this latter work have appeared in English translation to date). At the same time, this book marks a new approach in his work and in Russian literature in general. Indeed, while Russian reviewers have acknowledged certain antecedent practitioners of idiosyncratic prose-poetry within the Russian tradition, such as Aleksandr Blok, Boris Pasternak, and Osip Mandelstam, they have also noted that the work is in many respects entirely novel. The poet and critic Aleksandr Skidan, for instance, has suggested that *Chinese Sun* introduces new rules of reading into Russian literature.

Chinese Sun often leaves rules behind altogether. Just as in the strange world of Andrei Tarkovsky's *Stalker*, the reader cannot rely on familiar signposts and conventions. Following the strange twists and turns of the text, he or she must go by touch in a dark landscape of language interspersed with flashes of light. The text takes on a life of its own, elongating ideas in some places and letting them subside in others. Things that "never happened" are seen. The work demands a kind of inattentive attention. While the semantic disintegration caused by the text's multiple movements can leave the reader gasping for air, its twisting currents become a focal point so that the texture of the writing becomes the subject of contemplation.

Early on, the author neatly describes one of the effects of reading the "novel":

> "I thought," you said with some animation, "I was just about to understand something when it immediately slipped away, leaving my memory with a trace of delightful anticipation."

One anticipates understanding, but then finds that the text leads endlessly onwards and outwards in an erotic extension. The text constantly teases the reader with the possibility of fulfillment through both hermeneutic comprehension and sexual consummation. At one point, the revelation of a "blazing yellow ... sun" comes together with a "hot hand ... resting on my thigh," but the sun of the title remains mysterious and the sexual act deferred. The book maintains an erotic balance between moments of sensuous experience and vivid apprehension, and of incomprehension and loss. Oscillating between Eros and oblivion, the text leaves the reader with traces of this "delightful anticipation."

There is a visceral pleasure in reading Dragomoshchenko's prose, in which disjointed and endlessly changing experiences are enacted in the strange, disjointed movements of the sentence. The oscillations between focus and lack of focus, combination and disintegration are mesmerizing, swift, and playful: "Every tree seen from afar is a careless drawing in the margins of a notebook, even if it's meant to play a central role in proving arbitrariness."

Dragomoshchenko's work asks the question: how can something be "central" if it is marginal and arbitrary? The logical contradiction here is circumvented by the movement of the prose. The ability of Dragomoshchenko to seamlessly integrate apparently marginal and arbitrary details resembles John Ashbery's technique in *Flow Chart*.

Dragomoshchenko, however, employs a method that differs from Ashbery's approach in important respects. He utilizes contradictions, impossible combinations, and instances of sudden apprehension and vivid description to provide a startling counterpoint to the irresistible forward movement and ceaselessly shifting subject matter of his prose. Such moments of excess are often associated with sparks, flashes and other sudden impositions of light, which frequently coincide with moments of vivid memory, or "flash backs." Memories of childhood, in particular, recur in the work. This use of light as a marker of moments of memory might suggest romantic or modernist epiphany, but in *Chinese Sun* these moments are provisional. Flickering rather than instantaneous and absolute, they prove ultimately impossible to convey in language, except as intermittent points of light that punctuate the textual flow.

The overwhelming movements of memory, text, and parataxis intertwine to make the reader attentive to the functions and construction of self-knowledge and the work at hand. Dragomoshchenko's use of childhood memories recalls the work of Hejinian, whose book *My Life* intersperses childhood experiences and commonplaces with other texts and comments on the writing process itself.

As Dragomoshchenko himself has acknowledged, however, he does not use overt formal devices of the kind that Hejinian frequently employs. There is no strict formal structure in *Chinese Sun*, which is essential to the ebb and flow of Dragomoshchenko's linguistic effects; there are no obvious formal handholds because the mind knows no definitive structures but moves according to its own unruly caprice.

At one point, near the beginning of *Chinese Sun*, an occasion is recalled when a child—perhaps a certain Dragomoshchenko—experienced something indescribable. The moment concerns the discovery of another kind of existence within the self:

> I began to feel in my being a possibly alien, yet endlessly enticing, form of a different existence, something I was yet to discover—or so I thought.

But this alien moment will not return. The child spends years trying to relive the experience. This moment seems central—if anything can be called central—to the work as a whole. The text constantly strives and fails to return to its own origins, to its beginnings in "pre-thought" and in "pre-writing," just as the child fails to recover his foundational experience of otherness. The revelation of otherness in the self is a central flashpoint in *Chinese Sun*—a moment of "touch," as Mikhail Iampolski has described these instances in Dragomoshchenko's writing.

Moments of touch, however, are rare and unrepeatable. Acts of communication are erotic and pleasurable precisely because they are constantly deferred and defeated. It is only in their non-becoming or non-being that something happens, and writing, for Dragomoshchenko, is non-being par excellence:

> But no matter how hard the writer tries to say everything at once, this task—on the one hand inconceivable, and on the other, understandable—in the long run presupposes only one thing: a failure, the notorious "not so."

Chinese Sun is the other side of writing—"the notorious 'not so'"—raised to a new kind of extreme. It is only in this emptiness of non-being that the fullness of Dragomoshchenko's writing can occur.

Evgeny Pavlov has described the act of translating *Chinese Sun* as an encounter that necessitates an immediate response from the translator, just as it does for the reader. In his formidable endeavor, Pavlov faced an almost insurmountable difficulty: how to translate into English a work that relies on the syntactic and phonetic peculiarities of Russian for many of its effects. Dragomoshchenko employs the inflected Russian language to create sentences of great complexity in which each thought extends outwards, unwinding in multiple, intertwining threads of meaning. As much as is possible, Pavlov has retained the length and weight of Dragomoshchenko's sentences. In English (an analytic language), however, Pavlov can only gesture at the smooth and perplexing movements of syntax in the original.

Despite the untranslatable qualities of the original Russian, Pavlov has insisted that translation does not diminish, but rather enhances the power of Dragomoshchenko's work. Pavlov has written that the experience of reading Dragomoshchenko's book *Xenia* was "enhanced a thousand-fold by the English translation." *Chinese Sun* is a work that in both its content and structure appeals to the reader's experience of reading as a process of transformation from sensation to perception and from experience to memory. Such processes of re-encoding resemble the process of translation between two languages. For Pavlov, then, the process of reading *Chinese Sun* is analogous to the act of translation itself.

The word "sun" occurs repeatedly in the text,

providing a point of reference for the reader, as the polestar guides the navigator. The sun, however, does not so much enlighten as dazzle the reader. Flashes of light lead to a negation of clarity (like an overexposed photo). The novel ends in the extinguishment of the sun and in a moment of oblivion. *Chinese Sun*, however, does not leave the reader in darkness. Rather, the effect is analogous to closing one's eyes after staring into the sun—an image is burnt into the retina, into memory. The text explores this trace that light and experience leave behind. A book about memory and forgetting, language and its erasure, *Chinese Sun* defies the norms of autobiography. The immediate is endlessly extended. Objects of contemplation become elements of description, of composition.

It would be tempting to say that what the reader will find in this book will depend on what he or she is looking for, but this would be to miss the point of Dragomoshchenko's poetics of trace. Instead, it would be more accurate to say that to forget what one is looking for is the starting point for reading *Chinese Sun*. For Dragomoshchenko, only in that forgetting does writing begin.

—JACOB EDMOND

Often they don't let go of the musical instrument even in water.

—Gian Francesco Bracciolini

I see the Error screens that come up every once in a while to be flashbacks to the love...

—David Hendler

THE PATTERN OF GRASS determines the contours of "future campfires". A "question" arises (and in just the same way it disappears; guilt has not been proven): do we know that we know, or that "the pattern of traumas determines the pattern of the future"? There were other questions too. " ", the echo of wandering eyes turned towards the source and mouth, to the outpouring of dark spirals twisting into tracts of slipping recognition. Remembrance is direct speech raised to the power of interminable obliqueness. At that time my life was carefree and dissipated. No matter whom we asked, no one could tell us the composition of dirt. We were the sum of mirror splashes, running water, clay silt, and heavy nocturnal words (we are you) on whose spherical surfaces the crystalline sweat of a file of moons stood out like an August wind marching through gardens. We counted days by apples. But we also watched them go bad, shrivel, rot, and disappear, casting a shadow of doubt on the numbers that, following the apples, silently revolved like silver morning books lovingly pecked apart by rooster beaks—books that gave off hot fumes of premonition and impossibility. Millstones of the unfathomable. There were many viewpoints on this subject. Every crystal included the next one in which the preceding was contained. A carousel flashed various objects before the observer; the goal was to guess their designation. According to one viewpoint, dirt was a conventional rhetorical figure necessary for some calculations (that still remain largely unclear) of the coefficient of ice burning in the lower regions of hell. Back then we were convinced that ice was white coal. One can't escape precision. Heat came to town like a child to your doorstep on a stormy night—look at his teeth, some say. Just look! What do they remind you of? What exactly? Stinging snow? Vinegar? The backwater mirrors are woven with the colored silk of skies, feathers, and burning plants. Voices of others were unheard for the air rushing through the labyrinth of hearing. Tornado and crunch. The crunch of the first leaf underfoot in July laid out the map of a journey; those returning from it were not the ones who had left. Despite the smoke coming from smoldering swamps, I deliberately mark the boundaries of the narrative by specific dates (the '60s, '80s, '90s; if one so desires, one could extend them further, pushing aside the conventional present by endlessly exfoliating the future that aspires to be negated by a still more rarefied future) in order not to lend universality to the described events, which would otherwise color the narrative into shades of dubious poetic timelessness. To be sure, universality doesn't fail to render judgments, and moreover, recollections, bewitchingly unnecessary, but one has to pay a lot for this. Well, sometimes it's not all that clear what exactly one does have to pay. Foreground and background shift in the optics of experience. Significance moves by inconceivable trajectories from the event to its constant shadow, intention. At the first stage we can exclude color. It wouldn't be hard also to exclude premonitions and copulative conjunctions. Being means relentless transition. The point of departure is as relative as dirt under fingernails, immortality, the crawling of maggots in a rotting heap, and the phosphorescence of the outline of objects that live in the burrow of consciousness.

It is preferable to write about something that never happened—childhood— or something that will never happen—death. Such are autobiographical traces (cuts). Traces of absence melting away on things. Such things erase themselves in the proliferation and echoes of names, some of which, if not most, are doomed never to be pronounced.

Previously, my existence spread into various spheres, and it did so in ways that weren't at all mysterious. I must have wanted it so. I also wanted a multitude of words. Today I can't say why I needed it. Stupidity comes as a belated consolation. To understand what they understand, in order to fuse, at the brief moments of soot-pure impotence, one's own voice with the voice of the Other, one's own silence with the silence of thousands of Others—that question also arises. Pathos is destructive. We shall hear this on the roof. When, for example, did Dikikh get up from the floor and go to the attic? Who is he? Does he have a toothache? Does he like children? Does he donate money for the erection of the Temple? Stepping over pipes of the manifold, pushing half-rotted linen strings away from his face, swallowing stuffy air, he walks toward the dim window that opens to the roof.

What year is it? What season? Who directs the ceremonies of season change? Dikikh put a box underneath the attic window, stepped on it and pulled himself up. Gray night air touched his forehead. Did his soul, charmed by the incarnation, really forget its prior existence? The flat roof of a six-story building stretched out in front of him. The silence seemed tinfoil-thin. How much is money worth? The tinkling didn't take up too much room. Does one need to know this? To the right of Dikikh, a middle-aged man in a well-tailored suit was seated comfortably in a chair. He wore light, tinted, rimless glasses; his nose was covered with tiny red veins. Standing behind his chair was a Chinaman with an open book in his hands. A light wind stirred the pages. A hat used for worshipping Good lay on the tiling by his feet. The star Red Phoenix was above the Vyritsa.

"I've seen all this somewhere," remarked Dikikh, arrogantly pointing his finger at the Chinaman.

"Is that a question or an affirmation?" The man in the chair gave him a friendly smile.

"I don't know how a question can be an affirmation."

"Well, I'm really not an expert on such things."

Dikikh sank down on the roof. Overcoming the onset of fatigue, he remarked, "the roof has warmed up quite a bit."

"No one," grinned the sitting man. "I'm positive, no one needs this. Above all, me. I'm a businessman, you see. I like things you don't. I like, let's say, to add one thing to another. You, no doubt, prefer something else." His voice took on a somber, operatic note. "Although you may like, for example, to steal... Not that I have anything against stealing! But to me that too definitely seems an exemplary case—granted, a pathetic one—of something that doesn't exclude gathering—right?—or, if you like, fullness, which, as you understand, doesn't care how much of it is taken away on each particular occasion."

"I understand," nodded Dikikh.

"No, you don't," said the man. "You understand absolutely nothing."

"Yes, I do," repeated Dikikh. "At least, I'm guessing."

"That's it!" interrupted the other. "Everything happens as if it were sleepy guesswork, a state, or, if you like, a place that can describe neither result, nor prerequisites. And you know, here's what's most important: this sleepy interest—perhaps, even indifference—has its origin in itself, in this very sleepy guesswork where nothing happens 'all of a sudden,' while the rest is merely a stumbling block that shifts guesswork from sleep to recognition, to the reality of the moment read... say, backwards, toward the point where guesswork again begins to approach its own 'all of a sudden', the incalculable part of somnabulistic curiosity. Believe me, there's neither a single affirmation, nor a single negation—that's what's remarkable."

Dikikh scratched one foot with the bare heel of the other.

Amethyst reflections glinted on the sitting man's face, on the lilac jacket of the Chinaman standing behind the chair, on the pages of the Chinaman's book, flying around with the crackling of torn crêpe de Chine, on the carpets with which the roof was covered. Dikikh walked over to the edge and looked down.

A yacht was sailing down the Fontanka—the same one he saw while moving to his new location, except this time its mast and sails were set. The yacht glided, enveloped by soundless tongues of cold flame. People burning on the deck waved affably and tenderly as they sailed by.

"You see, fire." The man in the chair took off his glasses and with visible pleasure held his face up to the reflections floating in the air.

"There's some vagueness in your argument. I'd like to eliminate it as soon as possible," said Dikikh quietly.

"Ivan Ivanovich," the man introduced himself and winked at Dikikh as if he were an old friend, a comrade from the good old days.

For some time, the man, already Ivan I., seemed to be deep in thoughts, his head bent as he was pondering the answer that apparently occurred to him. Then he stood up and leaned on the Chinaman's shoulder. Holding the book in front of him, the Chinaman uttered instructively: "Hearing is a step of courage, and the weak must not be admitted to it. Amazed is he, deep in the sea of contemplation."

"Yes, in the sea," Ivan I. echoed. "Precisely; not in some ocean or river. And the state of the sea is like the state of women who cut their hands with string while contemplating the beauty of fish. Remember, their amazement was so immense they lost the ability not just to feel, but also think."

At the end of September, Dikikh knocked on the door of a bathhouse in Fonarny Lane. It was early morning, around six. In the yard, behind a pile of pipes, a lonely linden tree was beginning to shed leaves. Underneath it were rusty wire chairs. The door gave way easily, which made Dikikh nervous. His footsteps resonated down the corridor. Having passed a plaster Madonna-and-infant, then a bear-and-border-guard, Dikikh stopped and yelled, "Who's there?!" There was no answer.

Dikikh moved further along the wall, trying to tiptoe. Of course, as you may have guessed, he had forgotten all about Ivan Ivanovich. Sand screeched under his soles. The repair time is described elsewhere with pertinent detail regarding the replacement of many units of the necessary pieces of hardware.

Then he heard singing as if coming from a radio. As Dikikh moved further, it became louder and more inspired. He passed a cafeteria, an empty locker room, and entered a room with a swimming pool filled with a great number of fish tanks in which exotic rainbow fish were splashing. The room was furnished very simply. In fact, there was almost no furniture in it, save for multiple doors adorned with brass nails and perforated carving. Some of the doors faced Ka'bah. Fragrant Grotta wood was burning in the hearth. One could only be dazzled by the fretted plaster of the walls... Pray, pray, oh Maghrebi, but don't look that way! The singing came from Vitya the Tartar who was diving and splashing in the pool. The regulars of this heavenly place knew him as Lombroso.

Vitya the Tartar gurgled and sang. He owed his nickname to the occasion when, breaking his own rules, he interfered with a conversation between clients discussing the nomination of some new figure for the position of the superpower's semi-head. "It doesn't take a Lombroso to understand what's what," Vitya had said and spat on the floor by his feet. Sometimes he swam to the edge of the pool, poured himself a drink from a bottle standing there, raised the glass to the light, and admiring the color of the contents, drank them slowly and languidly, then sang again. Up above, underneath the high vaults, echo's ghost was captured in the formula of intent smalt; in the pool, little schools of goldfish whirled in tiled indigo. Lombroso was an expert on many things, goldfish being no exception.

Dikikh returned to the locker room, crossed the corridor, entered the women's empty classroom, and opened the door to a utility room. A blue curtain on the window barely let through the dim autumn light. Dikikh went over to the trestle bed, knelt down, and took Sonya's hand. The hand quivered, but her face remained in the shadow of sleep. Dikikh took off his raincoat, put it over the blanket and lay down next to her. But as soon as his eyes closed, as soon as the violet spirals of the usual obscure suns started to crawl in them, gathering themselves from the seeds of the matter of vision, he saw again, as if through the aperture of a slowly opening door, a seemingly familiar room, a man lying still on a couch with his eyes open, surrounded by silhouettes as though bent over him.

This vision wasn't a regular visitor to Dikikh's dreams. But when it came, Dikikh's heart was instantly free from the feeling of senseless and irretrievable loss, which could apparently be explained by the unpredictability of what he saw, as well as by the ease with which the vision disappeared. Shaving the next morning he would always say to himself in front of the mirror that this dream (its part, a part of its part, and so on) is a purely accidental combination of disparate attributes each of which by itself must have meant something at some point in his life—or in the lives of others, for they could just as easily have been someone else's.

It's possible to assume, he reasoned, that the room could be one person's dream, the couch and the man on it another's, while the silhouettes surrounding the couch could rightfully belong to Dikikh himself. Taken together, however, everything became corneous gates through which a merciless wind of unknown origin was blowing.

The sum total is invariably perplexing, even though politics and religion have claimed to be the opposite of one another, apparently with much success.

I don't remember, I must have also wanted to be together, that is, in the same place with others, despite the fact that imagination still refuses to represent that place in any way. Once on the metro, rereading a short poem by Wittgenstein about the frozen sea and the dream of a shrimp, I turned my eyes away from the page and looked at the row of lamps flying backwards on the tunnel wall.

We are yet to reach the illustration in which someone in a tweed cap with his head thrown back stands holding the trembling string of a kite. The dim brass of the journey has grown into the skin of his hand. The aggregate of lamps resembled an infinite, enchanting ribbon on which an electric horse ran tirelessly, trying to get ahead of a tree that flew into the twisted perspective. Are twins the reason mirrors were invented? Could the knowledge that mirrors rule over us have given birth to the phenomenon of twins? Or could it be that twins are *mirat hadratein*, the mirror of a double presence, of divine readiness, an imperative—and of a possibility, a light foot, and an uninterpreted dream? Thus in childhood, in the darkness of summer nights, we used to spin lighted reeds around us (almost dancing on one foot like the Hassidim), savoring the illusion of the pattern endlessly changing in the air, of the duration of the singular, or perhaps simply of what is deliberately accidental, torn apart, disjointed, and doesn't obey the hand that for some obscure reason thirsts for wholeness. Who can say how deep, at the time, the hidden desire was to combine things that even to a child's mind seemed devoid of surface compatibility? Or was it the "sluggishness" of vision, the given fact of bodily imperfection the designation of which was precisely not to miss the experience of its further limit? The crowns of dark Sumerian linden trees flatly illuminated the boundary of in/ above. Every tree seen from afar is a careless drawing in the margins of a notebook, even if it's meant to play a central role in proving arbitrariness: thus arbor and equus in the rarefied sphere of arbitrariness. Geneva on the eve of 1908. Do me a favor, don't interrupt, but nobody's interrupting—yes, you are, you're always trying to ruin everything, trying to start a needless story about changing times, about the sale of rotten barrels, about carts on heavy iron-coated wheels, about a blooming chestnut tree at the corner, about something that hasn't been of any interest to anyone for ages; but what about then?—what are we to talk about when everyone's fallen silent, as though early morning has come, light is changing its tissue, and night speech, dying out in your memory, has been washing the desire never to stop, never to break, even for a second, because the break (sometimes it assumes the form of ellipses), and so on, something else—unnecessary—it's already broad daylight, somewhere behind back yards, by the river Okkervil a tramcar is clanking, while the tree by the window (an elegant turn of things, a tree appears—it's been appearing for quite some time!) loses its menacing sharpness, well-matched with the description that passes choice after choice in a somnambulistic tracing of its own traces discovered in the course of tracing; therefore, in part, "I still can't understand what was most important in our relationship; the fact that we continue to talk about it (no, I'm not trying to impose my opinion), as if endlessly descending into the kind of life where there's no room for words, into nether regions of language that ceaselessly dreams of the past, of someone's memory in order to find the one and only direction of desire, avoiding" requires a larger involvement in interpretation, and it's hence of little interest whether it's needed or not, although it and nothing else could become the cause of yet another sorting out of relationships at the end of the night when the room is full of people, when there's nothing left to drink, and the dissipating haze doesn't add clarity to your thinking, and you nonetheless keep returning to the necessity of talking about something else; I don't know what exactly is needed at this hour, can't you see birds being blown off their feet, water giving fruit, and the moon shadowlessly lashing down on the sea that marches to the city? I detest your excessively elevated tone. I can't listen to people who worry only about not forgetting what it is they want to say. People whose features contain *arbor* and *equus* as a seemingly unpretentious example, similar to that of a policeman collecting all possible data about local residents—an example in which the map of "nowhere" or "nothing" is played out as an additional factor of understanding. All examples are doomed to nowhere and nothing, same as "the Cretans", "plucked roosters", etc.; of course, the non-signification, the semantically neutral modicum of words introduced into the body of an example secretly indicate a conspiracy, a blind appropriation of meanings that puts in doubt the very measuring of, and reconciliation with something that by means of such likening unconditionally claims its indisputable place. "Why, it's as simple as...!"—the figure of example is the figure of comparison in differentiation. But as soon as it first starts to slow down, the "tree", notwithstanding the restraining power of its "roots", sprouts with sudden ease through the landscapes of reason and the synopses of Degallier or Riedlinger—it is I, a functionary of the double name, who doesn't remember distinctly when it happened—in order to accrete with the horse whose picture is given below as something obviously incidental, and hence typical, not at all categorical—but the thing is they weren't separate, didn't differ, the horse of Odin (Igga) and Yggdrasill. Here's probably the very spot where the flank of the Geneva reserve starts to give in. One could imagine further confusion. For example, the Odessa of that same time, 10th or 11th station, many lamps, crystal glasses, carafes, other objects on the table under a branchy walnut tree. Tussore is glowing softly, "Why yes, you were simply born to do this! Won't you manage? Don't be silly—if you get stuck, we'll help you. Gentlemen, I've a funny idea! But first, which of you is planning to depart for European capitals this fall?"

This, however, doesn't catch us unawares. Here's a comparison of dates: in 1906, the "tree" sprouts, while by 1908, it branches out maturely as an example in the rhetorical maze. Let's talk about something else. Let's talk about houses and fires that surface from the bottom of halted October days; let's talk about voids, about wax tablets of dreams to whose pliable matter an imprint arises, exfoliating, from the depths of yet another surface. Let us finally say—in that same year he leaves Berlin only to find himself in Derbyshire, England, lost in the soundless orgy of kites. Aerial horses of Ashvins are inescapable, horses of twins, of heavenly offsprings marked by the stamp of servitude. In his book, The Crown of Kings, Buhari al-Jawhari likens such a person's existence to the Diamond of Eleven. That same book wisely says nothing about the magic carpet guarded by kites, flying snakes of wax dreams, that is, by the dream itself, from the very beginning turned to itself, unto itself, avoiding any description. Procrastination is the first thing to master.

After this and that, nothing is left except "notebooks": in both cases scholars classify them by color—green, brown, black, blue. Finally, the notebook of water and smoke. It is no secret that not a single word is to be found in them about the fear Hippolytos had for his mother. Not a word because it wasn't misogyny, as one would expect, but apparently something else that filled him with insurmountable fear—i.e., him who actually was the horse to be sacrificed, dismembered, dissected into meanings in order to be newly re-combined in an impossible whole of a certain meaning—but does the ritual of *aswemedha* merely come down to murder? Let's not go on, let's leave it, ok, let it be so. Listen, you—excuse me, you, on the left from the window, the person marked by the street's turning to evening haze, thank you—what would you like to add? But then, you're saying even more quietly, with your whisper even closer to hearing (thus ivy on a wall sleeplessly clings to autumn), then they took the horse all around the kingdom, walked it through every domain, and the queen waited to receive all of its might at once, endowed with the fullness of all her land, all her treasures, possessions, name, power, and immutability. Only later was it time to concentrate on the act of dismemberment, atomization, dispersal through a sieve of sacrifice. All over pages of notebooks, in the monotony of ascent. And it certainly becomes clear what young Hippolytos was afraid of at night, as it's clear why he ran to the beach, to the sand intertwined with vines of ascending winds, to the sea, to the chariot (the sequence is important) drawn by his favorite horses, but, as an outsider unrecognized by them as their equal, he lost the essence of wood, horse, and example. Indeed, Vladislav Valerianovich, quite so: "Ortygia, the cradle of Artemis, the sister of Delos, thou shalt open my sweet song in praise of horses whose legs are like a storm." If you feed me dinner, I'll tell you who knocked out my eye. One could sculpt a young girl's head to infinity. Plenty of clay. Much wasn't considered due to thoughtlessness. One could spend the rest of one's life with monks, tending roses in a garden. *Heißt kein Sternbild "Reiter"?* Heroes settled in consciousness, fragmentarily. There is noticeable movement in the thicket. Achilles.

Yet he didn't like Rilke, preferring Trakl.

"WE HAVE CUT, WE CUT, WE WILL CUT!"

FORGET "CUTTING" AS A FEMINIST ACTIVITY; THE MOTTO MIGHT MORE PROPERLY SAY, "WE WERE PATIENT, WE ARE PATIENT, WE WILL BE PATIENT." BUT WE KNOW HOW TO LOVE MEN. SO WE LOVE THEM.* I want to sleep. My eyes ache. It must be the flu. Today I choose love for the Fatherland, aspirating one of its syllables (I won't say which), and flu. Tomorrow I'll choose a Persian kilim. For now, though, a cup of grappa, i.e. coffee, and before I shut down the computer, I'll send you this story—first, however, I should finish it with a few words of yours which came in quite handy when words seemed

---

*Note: Small caps indicate English in the original. (E.P.)

to have no place anywhere at all. Even though patience here slowly turns into passion. …THU OCT 6 19:19:22 MSD 1994 TO: …@COMPUSERVE. COM MESSAGE — ID: <AAWL1B KMJ0@HM.SPB. SU> ORGANIZATION: WORLD READERS/FROM: DIKIKH DIK@…SPB.SU /DATE: THU, 6 OCT 94 19:19:22 +0400 (MSD)/ X-MAILER: DMAIL (DEMOS MAIL V1.14A) /SUBJECT: TREE & HORSE.

Dikikh had been gazing out the window a long while. Behind him was a room. The room was furnished with things. The things consisted of many states or, perhaps, of consequences of their own origins—false anticipation had forced speech to turn to sources of desire. A catalog of things is attached: bookshelves, books proper, photographs with human visages, a map of Petersburg covered with colored pencil marks, for the most part blue and red (yellow was barely discernible). Each thing was labeled. The room was quite dark this time of year. It was spring. Airplanes were soundlessly falling upwards. An uncataloged, unknown bird was singing. There were also a few maps of other cities in the room. A pile of books was on the desk next to the typewriter. We shall list their titles. Not all of them. Some are much too long. What's the date of this photograph?

One wants to start talking about the briefness of naming. Silence interested Dikikh least of all. A character, an actor in a play. Yes, he was no doubt, interested in names and action. He thought, we think, that we think names are "derivatives of things", but *proper names* are empty seeds blown by wind—not seeds, rather, but their shells, cases pecked apart by bird beaks. He allowed swallows to move into his house. The chapter was to be completed with the introduction of one of the characters. Such was the feeling.

As everybody knows, feelings are to be trusted. At the end of the chapter, upon descent, one should have written: "Chapter 14". The war had been going on for too long as an illusion of evenness; it ran through Chapters Six and Seven as a somewhat dirty thread, and after a pretentious loop of historical parallels, returned to Chapter One where, for a while, it went into hiding. Burdock was in bloom, the air was filled with the heat of motley grass and the ringing of grasshoppers. But eat, drink, and be merry in your contemplation, lie with women and search for a source of moisture in their whisper, in their mouths, also don't reject my words, my brother, my husband, for there is no measure to the immeasurable, and my voice is too soft, born in fields of reeds where light itself, despite its source, is as somber as times forever left behind. The world didn't fit in the book strictly because the weather was nasty and the bad glue couldn't hold the spine together. They'd already had time to get used to the war because language was unable to describe its invisible changes that, if read, could have provided a picture of variation and foliation: the war could have been waning, which in fact meant its renewal but in a different direction, on an absolutely different plane, where its sound, interrupted by *fermatos*, infrequent but strong in the deepness of their absence, gradually became more powerful; as a result, the wood of decisions was covered with flowers of death lovingly fashioned from wire, old newspapers and cheesecloth, as well as other kinds of flowers. But musical terminology didn't exhaust what was intended for it; screens continued to accumulate what was later interpreted as events. Just as they didn't give out proper names.

In an early chapter, Dikikh had been wary of a new character. His intrusion proceeded in the framework of a strategy hitherto unknown to Dikikh: the character bore no conventional functions, looked quite listless even though his indifference hinted at something more than a mere desire to appear a surplus meaning to the ornament.

The character started to appear more often, bringing in disorder and a vague anxiety to the progressively orderly picture of what was happening, and revealing himself in complete indifference and aimlessness. And it was also obvious that the character had nothing in common with the war.

March came. Dikikh had gazed out the window for quite a while, guessing in which direction the changes in his room were headed.

His mind slowly and persistently excluded things the catalogs of which never leave our hands. A photograph of a thing is also a thing. A lost photograph of a non-existing thing doesn't always exclude the latter from the realm of the possible. Now the *bookcase* was called "as she kept assuring," while the *dust on a Weimar wooden box with a metal cover decorated with a geometrical ornament* had the name of "this man shouldn't be going to Ibarra, he'll perish there". Substitutions failed to satisfy. The character indirectly announced his last name. It was terrifying. This is how matters stood. Dikikh never took his eyes off the window. He held his breath listening to the conversation— someone else was there. Dikikh had deliberately asked someone he knew at the post office to ring at a certain door (his own) and to give the person who'll answer it (himself) a fake telegram.

"A telegram?! For whom? Wait, I'll get dressed…"
"A telegram for Dragomoshchenko," said the mailman. "Does a Dragomoshchenko live here?" "Yes, I live *here*. Yes, *I* live here, if one could be certain of anything at all these days." "Sign here."

Through the half-open door Dikikh saw a hand with a pencil, a hallway, then a room with its door wide open, which may well have signified its complete absence. Simultaneously, as if looking from behind, one could see from the corner of one's eye a barely focused image: the silhouette of a woman leaning over a table, the gilded edge of a vase with swirling sun in it, a vaguely defined signet-ring, a blurred yet strangely salient (like the cool sky this time of year) house across the street, squeezed by the time of comparison in the evening space where the noise of cars rounding the corner never changed its direction, all of which was part of the phrase, "you'll enjoy comparing this to accustoming oneself to the limits of the room, the transparent limits set by each thing looking for its own extension in its own self-identity".

There were probably no other rooms in the apartment, despite a large number of doors adorned with brass nails and perforated fretwork.

Someone was lying on an unmade bed. I don't like it here, thought Dikikh, despite the magic abundance of light incommensurate with the amount of silver in the fixing solution. A curtain was flapping onto the window. I'll call the wet, sun-warmed spring air "remembrance". I'll get no penalty for it.

"Vera," yelled Dragomoshchenko, "give me some money... For the telegram!"

Dikikh heard a woman's voice, hoarse from a cold, "Who's it from?"

"Give me money, I tell you, don't give me 'who's it from'!" said Dragomoshchenko.

A theater curtain was flying down from above. And a stork. A sack was flying, a stone was flying into the sack, scissors were flying toward the sack. Where did the spring warmth, the light, the beautiful voices disappear to? People were moving toward the exit. Red letters of salvation. Nonsense, thought Dikikh, but immediately changed his opinion and thought that he needed a proper name, it didn't matter what would stand behind it (at least for the moment). Nor did it matter that the new character, formerly unemployed, lived in Tchaikovsky Street, closer to Liteiny Prospect, near the well-known passageway to Furshtadtskaya. At that instant, Dikikh suddenly became convinced he'd just struck good fortune. None of our business.

Dikikh saw Dragomoshchenko move along University Embankment alternately singing, dancing, and merrymaking. One couldn't make him out in three dimensions—he was most probably: 1) round-shouldered, 2) heavy, 3) dishonest, 4) mendacious, 5) bald and sentimental, all of which, according to Rudolf Mestsanger, indicates a dirty and unsettled imagination. Thus, Dragomoshchenko once noted that he is often taken for a Greek (yes, a Greek, not a Jew), but not always—still, why does the name Teotokopoulos come up in *Xenia*? The next step must be at some distance from theological interpretations. Is it the hardening of the affricative or of the faringal consonant that causes it? It was quiet and stuffy in the room. In the airless hallways, it "was". And how! The world's monochord was silent. The unknown character's movements were to follow certain hidden instructions. A question ensued: hidden from whom? From everyone without exception? Or will Dragomoshchenko alone and none other know, and knows already, what no one else knows? Another thing is possible: D. is apparently ignorant, but later, or rather after a certain time (compositional expenditures), or in the course of unexpectedly occurring events, he begins to guess the meaning of his own actions, i.e. movements. It would be natural to assume that as a result D. becomes suspicious of the scheme's coherence. Is the suspicion justified? I don't know. Where from? From a neighboring village. Does anyone look from above, reading what takes shape in letters, in his footprints? Does the meaning of the message depend on the location point of the possible "reader"? Furthermore, how many points are needed for them to become a line? Finally, what sort of a message or missive must be formed by such, dare we say, writing? There are several attractive suppositions.

Dikikh closed his eyes. He imagined that the movements of some D. could become meaningful if one followed him for 25 years. Dikikh became dizzy and felt a sour, nasty nausea. Let's assume he leaves the house, crosses the street, buys cigarettes, walks as far as Chernyshevsky Prospect, then returns by way of Furshtadtskaya. How did he arrive at the decision to do that?

By chance, as all people do. But what was his name? What do you care? What sign is formed? An incomplete letter "O"? Or a fragment of a yet undetermined letter, "B" for example? What's the punctuation? What's the principle of separation? Also, why the conviction that Russian is to be used here? This actually doesn't matter. It simply can't be that the native tongue, the soul's temple, should have no significance! Are we really to be left with just the view of endless plains? What's behind them? What prevents us, for instance, from reading the contours of his movement along the embankment, including his descent to the water, as the letter *gimel* or *alpha*? Dikikh felt cold sweat on his temples: there was no water, no Neva, buildings closed in tight before him. There was nothing, except the "was". Bad company. A few painted concrete fishes adorned the children's playground. The situation was inexorably getting worse. Dikikh looked toward the University.

In effect, Dikikh continued to reason in the kitchen as he watched the coffee on the stove, we're dealing with an utterance that unfolds in bodily time, an utterance that appears, writes Dikikh, as a meta-anagram in which we're to find keys to the solution of history, whose riddle he'd been seeking for over a year, definitely with no clue as to what might contain it: circumstances, faces, their speech, their stories, coincidences, acts endlessly flowed into one another, not finding the salutary stumbling point that could pluck the moment from the step of all dates in order to form the ovary of at least an approximate meaning even in the most inconspicuous of such sprouts. It's quite possible that the problem, for the time being, will remain unsolved. Despite emergent new details, it is said that the character is moving toward the University. Let's be specific: toward the History Department. Of this no one has ever breathed a word. But then one shouldn't breathe words, one should speak clearly. Calmly and clearly. As if nothing happened. As if it's always been this way. And won't or will be again. At the same time, one shouldn't obscure the main idea but, on the contrary, emphasize it. But let these movements (as is customary in contemporary novels) be in fact the drawing of letters meant to be placed on top of one another, letter after letter, day after day. Haven't we achieved certain sincerity this way? A character must have no particular occupation, so that nothing might affect the freedom of his intentions. Intentions owe nothing to anything.

We'll read what's not meant for reading, what will, in turn, sink to the depths of the utterance, of disappearance. These depths have neither a top, nor a bottom, but hover beyond the limits of physical attachments. Depth as the sky that isn't there. Then, with relief, spent names are listed, as if we didn't possess them, as if we existed as pronouns. Which will happen much later.

Night walked on without a splash: there's someone who crossed waters like dry land! In my room, the voices of mother, father, and guests displaced incidental shadows, like shaky islands of tender upheaval, in my room; the windows, as usual, re-composed the dusk. Beyond the edge of unclear voices, a steady, dull noise rolled on; back then, the sense of its wave-like approach used to bring a particular pleasure. It was as if you were nearing the threshold of sleep, the ivory gate that immediately expelled you back, into the anticipation of the blissful instant of transition, transformation, into the moment containing (in a triple exposure) the unfulfilled past, the already actualized present, and that which was just about to enter itself on enclosing the all-reflecting nexus of time, or the absence of the word that signifies this possible *never* radiating in all directions in a luster of incredible blindness and omnivision in which no means are left, only aims and which always remained an anticipation of that same past that never happened. The sequence is familiar: first, parents catch up with you, then disappear, leaving you to your own appearance, then you create your parents disappearing in their last return to you.

Was I the continuation, the source, the beginning of the noise—or of the voices coming from down below? The day's majestic yet helpless and pitiful world unhurriedly turned its gigantic disk, lengthened shadows, re-drew contours. Grass is straight, it stretches in a stratum of ochre to the borders of consciousness. As if for the last time (every night in a new approximation), with a strangely groundless and sentimental feeling, I touched sunflower stems, rough fence boards, apparently pressed myself to the tangible, balsamic odor of dry chamomile, dried fish, and, dissolving in it, fleshless and unconquered by space, moved on to the brass tinkling of window pane, studying the membranous, mother-of-pearl stamping of French perfume, the curvature and speed of a light ray, of printer's ink, the ice of playing cards, the keys of the Blüthner grand piano. Pubescence. Carpets revealed spirals of Sufi precepts, the bony hornet of porcelain buzzed by the teeth, splitting molecular conjunctions of walnut dust, while behind the windows, a high water of cabbage butterflies, whitewashed to cinders by midday sun, flowed like the dry waters of the Koran. These butterflies—I'm now quite certain—will never leave that time, just as the silhouettes of train engines never for a second leave de Chirico's potato clock dials. The origin of a child's love is at the center of the galactic giddiness of absolute loneliness. Soot. Calm clarity knocks you down: the landscape is a dictionary where silkworm nests overflow with the vanishing of the touches that make it—and of yourself, with your fingers dipped into the frosty fire of your shadow.

Numbness courses up the arteries in bubbling spurts.

In reality, the roots of anything at all hang in emptiness. The disciplines of vacuumology and virology are bound to explain Being. And this gift, unflinchingly waning with years, baring, like the low tide, the unsightliness of the recognized life's inescapable bottom, is the only gift that you try to share with others—unnecessarily, it turns out, because no one's left in the perforated cells of cancellation. But what is "then"? A vague indication of a time bound to happen, an actualization, or a brief, gratuitous nod backward, toward something "there", in the posterior: "then"? What produces *then*?

This ability declines with years, and at the next high tide, you enter it liberated from all that stood between you and nothing (then). Insects whose wings are covered with straw-colored inscriptions are dry and unsightly. Gulf, islands, snow, stone assuming any shape. Impossible—to convey the terrible desolation and boredom of winter nights in the deserted streets of the city where you spent your childhood. A frail electric light of bare lamp bulbs somewhere above, lilac dusk, snowflakes, the tapping of frozen branches in demolished acacia mansions. Neither shadows, nor darkness.

I was invited to talk about the secret laws of the alphabet, about five-year cycles of a gradual disappearance of letters from their positions—a phenomenon known to no one because they who (for no apparent reason) use the alphabet for their own purposes obsessively continue to operate with non-existing letters as though nothing happened and as though what stretched out before them wasn't a colorless, timeless, dimensionless desert, but instead what they call (resorting to supposedly known signs) a perfect silence where all meanings of future emergence and disappearance are simultaneously found, including the very meaning of the alphabet's endless, repeated vanishing. A chorus of mutes. History offers us more than names. Meteorites seemed like sparks flying out from under steel edge being set on the black circle of night. Same old dream keeps haunting the poet: speaking, he implies something else; thinking, he pronounces the opposite. The difference of rivers, flora, and fauna. The poet presses fingers to his lips (this gesture is usually perceived as a sign of silence) and tries to stop their predatory tremor because he fancies he's gaining an unmediated grasp of other forces and tensions—but the dream is lost in something else where it's all spent on some mysterious transformations no one cares about. Machinery of precisely measured interruptions. Naïve questions bring back the usual headache. On such occasions aspirin is useless. The pain resembles a prism where the monotony of what's always already happened undergoes a spectral split. It doesn't subside with years. Where is "always"?

I always used to start my story with this question whenever invited to talk about sacred laws that set in motion millstones of letters. As I said, it's there that one finds a gulf, islands, snow, a stone, and later, much later, a coastline curled in a snail of summer heat testing the purple and ultramarine underneath the wind-stretched net of myopia. But there was nothing worse than waking up at six (school started at seven). Once, however, I experienced a phenomenon that had nothing to do with my regular life: there was mild frost and a light snowstorm; I left the house as usual, about ten minutes before classes (the school was only two blocks away) and in half an hour found myself at the train station, or rather, on a street that led there, at the other end of town. At night, in bed, I tried again to penetrate the gap of the temporal rift I had faced that morning. Time after time, my imagination repeated the entire chain of reality's marks: breakfast, leaving the house... I saw snow swept away by the ground wind, I felt its incredibly piercing touch on my face, I smelled frozen dirt knocked off the sidewalk, I weighed and multiplied details to distraction as I began to see in them further evidence of reality. Despite all my efforts and perseverance, I couldn't reconstruct just one moment—the only inconceivable point of losing "consciousness", the point of "transition" that was meant to be something like doors—but doors to where? To the burning spark, to the moment of self-discovery? How did I spend those twenty odd minutes? Where was I? Who was I? A regal, boneless snail hovering in the purple of maternal waters? But how long was I, full of speechlessness and the quiet laughter of Bodhisattvas, destined to ascend to the mirror surface beyond reflections, names, and the voice? As Father Lob will put it much later, "neither human mind nor human aspirations can contain the divine smallness of this point; it won't fit in either intention or memory." On a chilly October morning, we'll sit on the roof of a soon-to-be-demolished building, scrutinizing the glasses in our hands and the ant-like swarming of Sennaya Square down below. Memory retained nothing of this absence. Does it mean I was really absent? Where? Why? Could it be that I passed out while continuing to walk, inconspicuously crossing waking streets? Perhaps I calmly talked to passers-by about birds and fir trees.

"In reality, there are only two questions between which our imagination hovers." We'll hear this from Fr. Lob, once known in the world as Aleksey Lobov, system programmer and later, with God's help, also hacker: "Will I really die?" and "Did I really live?" In their symmetry, these questions are fundamentally meaningless, as any questions for that matter, but any answer upsets their mutual equilibrium by endowing them with unnecessary meaning. What remains? "Then"?

I lay in bed feeling a chill on my face. Until then I hadn't yet encountered such unfairness. It was obvious to what extent I was hurt (or rather, insulted). God had always appeared in the scheme as a perfect algebraic egg, a topological incident forever drawn into literary circulation. What happened, however, branched out into something else. What happened that winter morning had neither place, nor time, nor definition in my vocabulary, nor did it bear any distant resemblance to anything in my experience. Nonetheless, it continued to exist and was now quite inseparable from myself. In other words, I began to feel in my being a possibly alien, yet endlessly enticing, form of a different existence, something I was yet to discover—or so I thought. But for years thereafter, waking up in winter with a joyful anticipation of a possible solution, I'd leave the house trying to re-enact every miniscule detail of that morning, up to the turn of my head, to the number of steps, to the thoughts flashing through my mind. I compressed myself into something like a tape worm, a ball, a figure of absolutely patient expectation (I only needed to understand, nothing more: I really pursued nothing further), freezing, losing myself, turning to ice with rage, yet remaining where I was, in the street, under the gray sky, behind the wall of useless and completely transparent eyes. All my subsequent life was partly composed of the same, irreversibly doomed attempts to approach that long gone morning: books, women, journeys stretching their power far beyond things and dreams, pain that, as it later turned out, doesn't belong to man at all, even if it "originates" in him—just as anything else that maintains a precarious balance on the brink of the verbal effort in whose stream, and in spite of whose intensity, imagination seems an empty pea doomed to an endless dance in the self-delusion of weightlessness and endlessness. It's not pain that belongs to man, but only its illusion, the suffering he appropriates as greedily as everything else. And so, if you practice the use of battle chariots, you'll advance in the right direction because innocence will vanish when you contemplate cheekbones and accurate moves. Anything could attract attention. Window frames, dried fruit prompting whimsical outlines of the nameless, lenses rotating transparent fields of authenticity on the ray threads they have spun. Human odors get stronger in the rain. The optics of knowledge have nothing to do with vision: there's no knowledge in the field of vision, just... an interrupted joke, some nonsense—there emerges a commune of Gurdjieff's worshippers, eucalyptus forests on brown coastal hills between Los Angeles and San Diego, yet the investigation starts in the south of Russia where she was last seen among a sect of flagellants—but anyway, all these hasty images are caused by none other than the sum of interconnections between white and black. A temporary truce sets in. Color emerges from its own absence, like the arriving reality of all sorts of "I's", "you's", "eucalypti", "realities", "relations", and so on. Whence the powerlessness to reject all this? What lies in wait under this layer? Just the awareness of a certain machine living according to laws that aren't your own? Hard to believe. But this very "machine", what is it? A conjunction of a few laughable metaphors? Perhaps, a mere vacillation between doubting the machine, resignation before it, and, of course, rebellion against it. A squeaking door.

During the day, a mirror propped against the wall by the door diminishes me and my time. At night, it leaves its simple tricks and breathes in barely trembling clouds caught by moonlight in the stillness: "Several lives go on inside me, but there's no place for me in any one of them. I think you know this feeling well. I think everyone knows it." On careful observation, as if penetrating the film of the eyelids, mirrors lagged by the smallest fraction of anticipation, showing that the matrix of shadows had the nature of liquid crystal. Insomnia's pollen drifted into the gaping expectation of capturing, grabbing the reflection of what generated it—it was the dust of the doubt as to what came first. Whether you liked it or not, only an exchange, a transition, a de-substantiation of the formation appeared essential. You don't sleep at night, choosing whispers as your guide; their cooled corners are blindingly indifferent and free from shadows—there are no shadows as there are no capital letters and punctuation. Is this really passion?

But the bewitching lenses of autumn! Numbers reflecting in round wells of matter, poets with emaciated mouths and hands convulsing with mutually erasing formulae, coal, white-hot reeds, and birds in crypts of limestone. It's impossible to forget what wasn't developed. Memory appropriates only that which determines the past—the body—it's as though the color were lacking, as though my hand drawing a line in the measured contraction of space "melted", spreading like an ink spot on wet paper, vanishing, first of all, in the laws of sensing its own corporeality, and then, in hoar-frost where one thing dreams of two but never crosses the threshold of the original. Yet, there is no return, and the ancient infant takes no pleasure in its joy—dry seeds, a flicker of cold October wind, an echo of voices belonging to nobody, as if the very "nobody" could ever be a belonging lifting a stage curtain, behind which a few dressed-up words dispersed in the play act out a simple comedy of jealousy, tickling, mirror, and makeup powder—or of the Big Bang and separation (is the infant its mother's erotic body?)—the sort one sees in a dissecting room. The removal of tissue, the barely suppressed surprise at the fact that the curtain conceals nothing—neither a dove, nor a worm, nor a gold coin, nor a "who are you?", nor a hunchback setting the automaton's meaningless little figures in complex motion.

The eye creates us.

We create the rest, which will be marked later by light pencil strokes.

One could make a choice: one could decide whether this is necessary, how urgently this requires that the narrative be continued with the introduction of recognizable lines of fate and voices melting early in the morning when you can hardly hear the beating of city stones underfoot and when those with a roof over their heads continue to see the enormous figure of justice dressed in many coats of oil paint. Or to cross out, send away, refer to fields of references, ant kingdoms of chirping eyelashes, to discard into the muttering brevier of shell rhetoric. Scales of dying. I didn't charm birds. Suspended matter falling out on walls of vision. Well, at least an ancient trick is finally explained: a kilo of down proved heavier than a kilo of iron used for bread, boots, and time. Later it turned out that the trees in the yard had all been cut down. After a while, the stumps, too, disappeared. There wasn't a sound coming from the downstairs apartment where, as long as I could remember, there lived an idiot with his one-armed mother. Summer heat came and went.

One of those days, the idiot and his mother, half-eaten by lice and fleas, were taken to an asylum. Vegetable prices went down. Harvest time was close at hand. According to neighbors, medics were collapsing as they broke into the apartment. Both rooms were filled with crap piled up to the ceiling—it turned out the plumbing had stopped working long ago. Perhaps it didn't particularly matter to the tenants anymore. Everything was changing. The worm was dying inside the apple. The apple the worm had carelessly chosen for his universe was dying too. And it was also clear that choice was out of the question. Too shallow, dumb. Light clashing with light, darkness with the same darkness. Yes, I know, one forgets words, otherwise why would I be writing this? Imprints smolder on the eye's retina. Is the eye an animal? Or is it a fruit, a berry, an algebraic egg that has nothing to do with the body? Or a wall enclosing memory? Perhaps the other way round. Even better. Now sleep. It snows. We are camping in Himalayan foothills. Tap water. Immortality's over. The snow passes. Many people. Fewer. Not too many, but not too few. I loved you. Love is incompatible with the present tense. What was that line? How should

I know? Of course: the banality of *everything* is first of all explained by the inexplicable banality of death. No, not like that. The banality of "everything" is posited by the inevitable "concurrence" of all possible explanations and circumstances in the point of "consciousness-death", as if it were sleepy guesswork…, as if in a dark boat among rustling leaves.

The dream seemed an extension of anything to which mind and imagination turned. Swarms of midges burned in emerald sparks; instantaneous, flickering encounters with a different matter diverted candle light from the straight axes of darkness. Absent-mindedly moving the fork on the tablecloth, his eyes fixed on his hands, father says,

"Indra's necklace." The ring burning on his fourth finger goes out without smoke. Yes, quite so.

"What were you saying?" Mother is seemingly caught unawares, she shyly tidies her hair—as if releasing the gold, all the gold in the world, from the light drifting out through the kitchen window into the yard as from something superfluous, excessive. Do you see her clearing the table? The picture starts moving, but how hopelessly empty it is! I see it. You see it, they see it too. I also see her straighten up and listen. *Who* is she? Who is *she*? Intonations. First of all, one should sort out intonations. You yourself just called her... I'm not saying no, I'm not saying yes, but I'm talking about something very different... Enter Vassily Kondratyev. He is drunk and sad. Under his armpit he holds a book, heavy as Heaven. There is no book in that book. "Like an appearance...," he says; nothing else can be made out. And no one exists except they who are falling endlessly into mirror specks of the deceptive surface, except splashes of dim light with its sharp wind blowing toward some indistinct substance.

"Yes, that's it. Indra's net," father repeats, lowering his shaved head.

We move in a circle. For a short time we find ourselves in the shadow of an apple tree, an eclipse, a new moon, cold hair, water, blood, and leaves. As if there was nothing, as if you and I haven't read all this! As if we were both then and now. But guess, then, where is now? Where is the cradle of adversative conjunctions? To what spaces do we move from what spaces while remaining motionless rocks, our own back-breaking load? "Does the minute of desire turning into a few drops of sweat on your bitten lips, into your moisture, my sperm, into this particularly magic touch of the hands— does this minute really enclose all without exception (because it all disappears): empires, durations unacceptable to reason, understanding, crunching bones, impotence, howls, ditches filled with limestone, shame for the desire to be at any cost (is it in our power? what nonsense!), us ourselves, and all kinds of gods viewing themselves with bewilderment as they depart from our limits, question mark. Intonation.

What does it cost then if, in the blink of an eye, it all crumbles—without even leaving the knowledge of that which burns to cinders what goes under the name of reality, arrogant in its invulnerability? Not a penny..." The lengthy monologue is unconvincing and requires re-writing for two voices.

We look hard for a second voice. The Other doesn't exist. We give speech to dogs, clay, minerals, God, sea-weed, and elementary particles, as well as them who open the door of awakening.

Speech (taught by itself) seeks the Other as a limitation that allows its return (representation of the circle it describes often preconditions the thought of wholeness), but since it never happens, speech becomes the weightless execution by correspondences of all through which it passes, shifting along the endlessly increasing distance, despite the abundance of omens and signs, the number of which would appear to be a guarantee of its authenticity. Excellent.

Wait though. What was I just talking about? What question was I asking you? But afterwards you turn and don't see the chair—was it an illusion or is it this: an illusion that continues to be such, becoming in you, winning you inch by inch until it turns you into its own absence? (Indeed, one can't really observe an abyss of that sort for too long). I assert: there was a chair here. No, there is a table here crammed with victuals. Leave it, I don't need any more wine. Better throw a blanket over my shoulders. How many times do I need to repeat: it's autumn. Did you think this season would catch us by the Great Ocean? Strange, it's been nearly forty years. "I couldn't find your traces anywhere." That's because there weren't any, as there was no you or anything else of which I, according to many, am a trace. Incomprehension is only an artless snare of love passion... its ears, eyes, nose, mouth are in the service of life. This is why they are to be governed. Upon completion of the course, appropriate certificates are issued. From them—and from the passage that follows—it appears that "language" seeking the Other becomes autumn whose dimensions include the becoming of each thing. What remains of a thing after it completes its cycle?—a residue of durations, vague indications of the cardinal points—but their number also depends on who intends to look at them, and how. Perhaps we've only one thing left: look at one another and keep swapping places. FATAL ERROR 404.

Mother straightens up, her left hand touches her hair. She looks out to the garden over her shoulder. The photograph slips down to the floor. There is no we. Mint, darkness, splashes, fragile ligature of floral life, threads of silk on sand spits, irises and peonies.

"I don't understand why he never completes his thoughts..."—this with fake bewilderment and no connection to what's been said. "Surprising, nonetheless, what he contents himself with—he who really appears to be a serious scholar. On the other hand, I think you'll agree that, regrettably, he's right on another point: language indeed suspects its own finitude, which requires the introduction..." Here one should obviously stumble, realizing the irrelevance of one's monologue. One should lower one's head—he does so—astigmatism; that we know: closer to the table to take a myopic sip from the shot glass, to sit back. Psychological literature must operate within the rhetoric of detail, of the *singular*, the *different*, of that which continues every possible mental presentation the reader may have. Why doesn't he complete his life? The shot glass, the description of ostensible behavior, of conditions that expose the character's behavior. An example: Dikikh thought he was thinking. An August night wind slowly rolls through gardens. Mathus Izraelevich Mann follows his grandfather's example and, wiping his mouth with a napkin, addresses mother,

"Well, time to go, it seems. I wonder what time it is."

"Oh, not late at all! Stay with us a while longer," says mother, smiling to father while also trying to take his fork away from him.

"Yes, I'm sorry," says father, "silly little habit."

"Kondraty Savelyevich," Mann turns to father.

"I'm all ears," he replies.

"Well then, are we going mushroom picking on Sunday?"

"Yes," I hear myself say as I look out the window where the same nasturtium is in bloom, and the northern sky spreads the sweet lie of yet another change of season. Utensils of affirmation.

"Great, but *absolutely* no one has time to mend the boat!" grandfather fires up all of a sudden as if finding at last the long-awaited use for his expectation. Who has ever seen nut-tree fishing rods—not your ordinary kind but collapsible ones, with joints made of rings cut from cartridge shells of various caliber? But now, in a fit of theatrical irritation, one could, on the quiet, down another shot of liquor.

"Father, but you promised!" says mother.

"Ah, Masha, tell them to bring in some more golden wine (he laughs as if he'd come here from a distant land). You're a golden treasure. If they bury you, they won't think of unburying you."

"Tell me please, why do you have two identical epithets shamelessly in a row?" asks father.

We are not there. The development of production forms changed forms of perception. Seashell formation also changed. Perception changed lingering images of emerging and alternating details. "Tell me, are we ever going to screw like normal people, in bed, with sheets, for real? Are we doomed always to do it like this, in bushes, attics, kindergartens, boat sheds?" In the hills. After an eternity, a magic mountain appeared. A typewriter on the cupboard proved to be coincidence incarnate. Eternity doesn't always mean "always". With what did a letter coincide when it tried to find itself in the blissful inarticulateness of premonition? Everything happens by itself for those who are empty and free at heart. Twins. And after some more unregistered time, Grandma, with her eyes staring like chalk birds smashed by a snow-storm, will tell me that Mann "died very nicely, may God have everyone die that way", i.e., in his sleep, with face turned to the wall. Deep breath-ing. Such is the pneumatic plot. If he is right, he is calm. No use existing according to a different archeological object. I don't know the meaning of the latter word. Does an imprint fill emptiness, or does it form it? Azure paint should be applied to an article with a careful and skillful hand. Is a sign an imprint? Is it a river? It's been a long time since I lived in these parts. In my absence, others didn't live here either. The room was a mess, it stank of stale beer. "Episode" and "fragment" may inter-sect on some plane if one doesn't accept their con-ventional limits. I was the only one to notice light flickers of their disappearance. They didn't disturb the flame of a single candle.

Sleep was sprayed on every surface, it en-dowed surfaces with insurmountable intransi-gence, turned them into something like a set of negations. Each of the negations was to disprove the one before and the one after it, but their sum total, as the sum of silence and voices, sometimes prompts the mind to ponder the probability of transgressing the vanity of expectation. A glittering wall of water was falling over me. Red-finned fish dashed in its depths while remaining mysteriously still. As I turned my eyes away from the lamps flying backwards on the wall to a stout middle-aged woman with heavy shopping bags by her feet, I thought that such a place is allowed only as a condition of a possible relation to it. And that one always finds it already removed before consciousness begins to "approach" it. At the same time I thought that the consciousness of such removal forces thought to seek the place of absence where it doesn't exactly vanish, but... Never imagined skunks could be so beautiful. And then came an opossum. This summer flung a sack to me across the wall. In it, bones of heat are clanking like a tram-car. The moon will pay for everything. The main thing is to slow down. But what do I expect to find in a place that's literally the *non-presence* of a place? A place not "occupied" by any of the people I know, shreds of whose conversations relentlessly twine round my head from the inside? Words, it goes without saying, no longer belong to anyone; consequently, they have lost their meanings—crystals of intonation twinkle in them with a thin coating of sense. These intonations add up to what satisfies the mind that hasn't left a single gap between itself and the line which weds absence to the intention of comprehending this absence as a reality, as *being*, as one of finite regions into which my existence should be spreading while realizing the falseness of its own aspiration. Beyond that, thought had no operational space, as it were. It was caught in a situation of immediate resignification. If I'm not mistaken, Wittgenstein's question was as follows: does a hole coincide with its outline? A frozen shrimp, water to your ankles, summer snow at night.

The middle-aged woman smiled and nodded towards her bags as if saying, there, that's how it is every day. The easiest thing to assume would be that if I asked myself the same question, I could ask, does my death coincide with the outline of my existence? If so, with which of its versions? I gave her to understand with a reciprocal nod that I agree—no objections there, "indeed, that's what happens every day". Of course, this vertiginous displacement within even more incomprehensible and abstract displacement could be stopped in an instant. But only if one took oneself seriously, including one's own body, or—as you'd say—past.

As is known, the process of growing one's corporeality is long and has no end results. To make it more understandable, I'll compare it to the process of acquiring language—on the assumption language existed before we "acquired" it.

Sometimes I smiled, imagining the simplicity of some phrase, such as "what are my deeds without God!" or "— — / — —!" Appearing from the cold haze of boredom, these phrases confirmed my belief that by continuously spawning dreams of wholeness, fear and narrow-mindedness hope to escape shame. Here one should speak of disgust. These phrases, heard frequently among others, always pleased me. But "understanding" is precisely the transitivity that existence denotes, or, to be more precise (as far as it's now possible for me), the latter's (but does it originate in "me" or *already* belong to me?) expansion, i.e., the place where it happens. And I can't say that I desire it badly. I saw generals colder than ice and harder than rock. I also saw them turn into turbid puddles of melted snow. It all depends on the climatic conditions and the nation's sexual orientation.

"In this picture, I am with mother.
I feel this is the end, he says."

What do *you* feel?

And, sensing it, I ask aloud: the end to what? Laughter is measured in liters. Then what was the beginning, and did they teach it as they teach, for example, driving a car or a hand—mastering, "putting on" power? Sometimes (but one could explain anything at all), I touch the photograph with my fingers. What do I expect to happen? On a vague impulse, I close my eyes, as though something should happen. The photograph is reminiscent of dried-up cheese. No, says the doctor, that isn't so. In reality, you're returning to the repressed memory of a snake devoured by ants. No, doctor, here I'm simply returning. Returning in an obviously phenomenological sense. From nowhere. Knowing, however, that I exist in the return. This is your Shadow returning to you. Not at all: we're removing the capital letter, and the shadow isn't returning anywhere already; moreover, it doesn't revolve. It stays motionless like a dry tree in blazing sunshine. We burn the shadow and warm our palms over its ghostly flame. Sometimes a snapshot can be compared to the end of September or to cuneiform engraved into clay that will never fall to shards by your feet one future winter. Thus we are young, full of energy, and are reading Dragomoshchenko. What is Dragomoshchenko telling us? Something about the length of stress in quantitative meters?

About spondaic, iambic endings? About dwarfs, unicorns, and mute princesses? About Yids and tender evening emotions? About being inexpressibly happy to live in a country that has chosen its own, unique path to somewhere? Alas, even given all his (dubious) desire, Dragomoshchenko won't tell us, or himself, anything new. The course of his narrative is known too well. It's determined, first of all, by fixed elements of meanings, and then by ways of connecting these meanings. Initially, he'll resort to the practice of piling up maxims that will become a manifest statement as they accumulate (this is how a certain E. put it once in a note to him while rewriting a fragment from *Xenia* in accordance with her own strategy of critiquing his writing). Then, about other things. In part, about the fact that I was denied my birth. Instead, I received the right to presence, which I never used. I know nothing about the rest—because I don't know who Dragomoshchenko is or who dreams of him in reading. There was neither "one", nor "many". For in whose imagination "his" image arises in the reading of the following sentence that says,

"I couldn't reach E. on the phone because there was no return address on the envelope. Perhaps, if I knew it, I could find out the rest—at least more than I know. I'd like E. to read this sentence and, if possible, what emerges after it. Further, I'd also like to hang from, say, a roof, squinting in the sun, and on seeing E. coming from round the corner, wave at her."

I don't know what you and I would talk about, but (at this moment) I feel something slipping and I feel I can't hold on to it. I am going to read aloud this still incomplete page as a letter to You that could quite possibly be viewed as a letter to myself because one couldn't think of a better occasion, even though imaginary conversations always feel vaguely like an action in which what one pronounces is from the outset opposed to the system of gestures accompanying or preceding (no difference there) the possible part of the utterance. As you may have guessed, I intend to speak about poetry. But as usual, as soon as I start talking about it, a multitude of other voices, audible and absolutely speechless, immediately start talking about something else—about beginnings, defeats, victories, incredible battles, expectations, and the words where speech addressed to these very words originates. Only one thing is absent from this whirlpool of inarguably enchanting logic and imagination: the possibility of stumbling on some perfectly meaningless question. I'd like to point out that I deliberately distance myself from the all-too-facile equation of answerability with the ability to answer, i.e., the ability to change one's nature in accordance with the question, or in other words, the ability to become the asking that comes at you. [...] you see, I deliberately reject the possibility of avoiding in rhetoric not so much the answer as the question itself—why I (if someone desires that what was said be addressed to him) at some point in my life made the attempt (as it turned out, a failed one) to find the pretexts or, if you like, "origins" of my predilection for the clearly useless occupation of combining words. AT LAST AS I AM SITTING DOWN WATCHING THE ROUGH EDIT, I WAS STRUCK BY THE NOSTALGIC TONE THAT SUFFUSES THE TEXT AND MUST THEREFORE HAVE SUFFUSED OUR LETTERS. AND IN RETROSPECT, IT SEEMS PARADOXICALLY PROPHETIC THAT WE EXPERIENCED "GETTING TO KNOW EACH OTHER" AS AN EXPERIENCE WITH THE PAST, SINCE, AT LEAST, IN YOUR CASE, THE WORLD IN WHICH YOU BECAME YOURSELF HAS SUDDENLY, IF NOT APOCALYPTICALLY, VANISHED. But I'm glad it's coming to an end—it would have been easier, of course, to know beforehand that our publishing venture (though even now I hardly imagine the entire story of our letters as *some kind of a novel*, albeit at different times, almost in a dream, I managed to see its several fragments) would finally take shape. MAYBE CULTURES—SOCIETIES—ARE ALWAYS MANIFESTATIONS OF THE PAST, RATHER THAN THE FUTURE. CERTAINLY WE LOOK BACK WHEN WE ATTEMPT TO EXPLAIN THEM. And this is not so much about "formal solution" (in which I habitually trust myself) as about its inclusion in a set of facts present in my experience and conceptions. "Book", "door", "wet shoes", "current legislation", "dreams", "telephone call", "beer", and so on, little by little become equal in the laws of their existence and for that reason relate to me to the same extent that I relate to them. What sort of relation is this? It would be easiest to describe it as a state of unstable truce. SO WHAT WE WROTE, WHEN WE WROTE TO EACH OTHER, WAS A KIND OF HIS-TORY. But returning to "letters" and to that time, I can only guess that the *annoyance* you developed every time you turned to them (WITH THE NOSTAL-GIC TONE, PONDEROUSNESS, ETC.) and the annoyance I had every time I remembered them later (which, I confess, was the reason I read the final draft more than absent-mindedly) is quite understandable. At least because a love letter (NOT A "LETTER" IN THIS CASE) is in its essence ambivalent. THAT'S VERY DIF-FERENT FROM POETRY. I REMEMBER (MORE REMEMBER-ING!) WHEN WE FIRST MET. BECAUSE OF SOMETHING YOU SAID (OR SOMETHING I THOUGHT YOU SAID) I WAS DRAWN

TO KNOW MORE OF YOUR WORLD, BUT THE WORLD IN QUESTION WAS NOT "RUSSIA" BUT "WRITING". YOU SAID THAT AS YOU WROTE, EACH WORD CHANGED FROM RUSSIAN INTO THE LANGUAGE OF ANOTHER WORLD. As an act of erasing the present, including writing, the latter produces a space of actual vacancy ("expectation", "anticipation")—it is this very "space" that becomes the sought-after "product" of writing, its "creation", "creature": *its reality.*

Or merely reality's possibility—that endless beginning to which literature is doomed *from the start* no matter what disguises it wears. The writer, if of course, he isn't "asking" for money, salvation, or compassion, can be compared to a person who, while trying to tell a story important to him, is constantly interrupting himself with some indistinct muttering, such as, "*no, not so, not like that.*" But what does this "not like that" mean? What does "so", what does "not so" mean? If not so, then how?

IN WANTING TO KNOW THIS OTHER WORLD, I NEVER THOUGHT OF IT AS UNRELATED TO RUSSIA—I KNEW YOU WEREN'T SUGGESTING THAT POETRY CONSTITUTES A FANTASY REALM, UTOPIAN OR OTHERWISE. NOR DID I THINK OF IT AS UNRELATED TO MY PLACE. NOR, FINALLY DID I THINK YOU WERE SUGGESTING A "UNIVERSAL" WORLD—FREE OF NATIONAL BOUNDARIES, LANGUAGE BARRIERS,

ETC. BUT I DID THINK OF IT—AND STILL DO—IN YOUR WORK AND IN MINE-NOT AS "THE REAL WORLD" BUT AS "THE WORLD BECOMING REAL". But as far as I know, this "no, not so..." lies deep in writing's every cell; it is apparently one of its principal motivations. What was the "not so" in our case? Our exchange on the plainest of words and concepts, apparently quite indubitable? But no matter how hard the writer tries to say everything at once, this task— on the one hand inconceivable, and on the other, understandable—in the long run presupposes only one thing: a failure, the notorious "not so". AND, CURIOUSLY, DESPITE THE EMPHASIS ON MEMORY THAT DOMINATED OUR LETTERS TO EACH OTHER, IN COMBINATION WITH THE IMAGES OF FUTURE WORK IT IS NOW NOT UNLIKE A POEM—A WORLD BECOMING REAL. In my latest book, *Chinese Sun*, there is a line: "It is preferable to write about something that will never happen—death, or something that never happened—childhood." Indeed, there seems to be no past. Individual facts held by memory in a particular sequence or chain, remain isolated facts extracted from a certain moment of time (this may be the origin of the mysterious, vertiginous charm and elusiveness they occasionally produce). Subsequently, something else *is becoming*: not facts themselves, not events, but the way in which they correlate with my/your current intentions, with my present desire, intent. WHEN WE WROTE TO EACH OTHER ABOUT "BOOKS", WE BOTH TENDED TO FOCUS ON OUR FIRST EXPERIENCES WITH BOOKS—OUR FIRST ENCOUNTERS WITH THEM, WHEN THEY WERE STILL STRANGE OBJECTS, ALMOST FORBIDDEN, OR AT LEAST ARCANE, CONTAINING INDECIPHERABLE INFORMATION, HIDDEN KNOWLEDGE—AND, OF COURSE, PROMISE. THAT'S FINE—THOUGH PERHAPS OBVIOUS. NEITHER OF US SPOKE OF THE MORE "TECHNICAL" USES OF BOOKS— THE WAYS POETS PLUNDER BOOKS (AND NOT JUST DICTIONARIES) FOR WORDS—FOR WORLDS THAT GATHER AROUND WORDS RATHER THAN EMERGE FROM THE VERY LIMITED IMAGINATION OF AN INDIVIDUAL. It's permissible to assume that the past, to some extent, also comes from the future, from its foretelling. It's as if we were moving towards something that had already happened. Strange recollections, strange intuitions... The reminiscences that at the time were part of our meditations were projected onto the desire to see/write both past and present (in which both we and the act of writing were located)—i.e., onto some detached future. In other words, we were adding the very project of the yet incomplete exchange to the same set of reminiscences. AND NEITHER OF US SPOKE OF BIBLIOMANCY—OR OF THAT WEIRD FORM OF IT THAT MAKES A BOOK, OPENED AT

RANDOM, SEEM TO BE SPEAKING OF JUST THAT IDEA OR OBJECT ABOUT WHICH ONE HAD BEEN THINKING. SO, FOR EXAMPLE, I OPEN A BOOK HERE ON MY DESK. IT'S "ERROR 404", A TEXT I AM TO TEACH THIS WEEK, AND THIS MORNING I OPENED IT AT RANDOM (AND, AS IT HAPPENED, AT PAGE 93), WHERE THE FIRST SENTENCE TO JUMP TO MY EYE SAYS, "NEIGHBORHOOD MEANS: DWELLING IN NEARNESS." THAT'S TERRIFIC! POLITICALLY—AND, OF COURSE GEOGRAPHICALLY—NEARNESS MAY BE DIFFICULT, UNLIKELY; ARTISTICALLY, ONE CAN IMAGINE THAT IT IS BECOMING INEVITABLE.

Days given to me, as days given to many others, were adding up by themselves, with no required effort on my part. I noticed, for example, that I lie involuntarily, inconspicuously for myself (and more often for others) not because of a fear of being caught in various transgressions, or because of an habitual emotion of which the fabric of our monotonous lives is woven, but because of a subtle, partially malicious pleasure of changing the correlation of things and the correlation of moments—in a word, because I desire to endow facts with the significance of events. As if the keys to these events' interpretation, or, if you like, understanding were in my own hands. "Lou, evil people sing no songs—why do Russians?" Oh, my poor head, alpine air clanking with coat buttons and steel eagles, pianos clattering in the gardens of Hesperides: "how could you have lived so long hiding such an exquisitely engineered design of your life?" If it weren't for the blueprints you left to your sister in upstate foothills, what would remain for us? A crystal vase? A hammer? Valium? In much the same way, the surrounding world tried to make me an accomplice, tried to drag me into its screenplay so as to make me believe in its own endlessness, in which its every lie invariably turned out to be true. Only I can testify about the Cretans. It was precisely a search for "truth" that I was to use as an instrument of knowledge. One remembers a line from Myamoto Musachi who was in the '70s surprisingly popular with the Soviet intelligentsia: "The sword is raised, the inferno is wide open, your heart is trembling with fear. But move only forward, and you shall find the land of light." Later, the intelligentsia was converted to *meekness*. In both cases—"towards oneself", "within oneself", etc.—there was a trap of some vaguely false challenge (how could we have forgotten holiness!), a challenge I, unfortunately, couldn't accept, preferring my own time in which the world sees itself as it is—reflected, as though in a dream, beyond the wall of my vision. Taking the thesis further, one could put it this way: if the world is dead, you must prove to it that you are a hundred times more so. Only complete indifference allows me to move fingers across the keyboard. An imperceptible displacement of a shadow on the ceiling. I didn't say I was writing—what I do is more like going over possible combinations and the speed of their displacement. Would it really be that crucial if at some point they managed to prove to me that he was alive? One shouldn't give too much to habits—liberation from them could be catastrophic. What's crucial is the measure of relationships. But this logic is obviously quite faulty and inconsistent. As far as the definition of measure is concerned, Death has no meaning. It's on its edge that we empty ourselves out. Stumbling, spilling everything on the floor. Parts of imagination. It's not only hasty, but also optional. So much the better. Like everybody else, I don't understand what I'm saying. Do I picture a "tree" in my imagination when I say the word that signifies it, or when I sink deeper into the slumber of the hand moving fingers on the keyboard? The sky behind me is shredded by lightning. I'm even inclined to say opened up. At the moment, this appears more precise. But how long will this moment last? And what does "more precise" mean in my case? Do I want to convey more fully the sensation I perhaps experienced when I noticed the gleam of lightning on the screen, or was it my utter inability to continue (idleness? weakness? indifference?) that got me to focus on a random observation? If to convey, then to whom? For what reason? How would I be able to describe (granted this is no description) imperceptibility? One has to admit that there is no tree. As there is no death. Because there is no picture, no image of either one or the other. What arises to consciousness in the reading of numbers? Other possible numbers? Perhaps the very last remnant from childhood days is the habit of measuring everything by apples, fingers, and pebbles. Similarly, I have to imagine myself the way somebody else sees me. If the somebody were removed, then one would probably experience oneself directly—so they say. But I understand nothing. I am an animal (justification). Or rather, a plant with caries-corroded teeth, tormented by the blind fear of being constantly present here or there, or short-of-here, or beyond-there. It's like groping in the dark in search of the familiar wall and finding nothing. The hand falls through. Sometimes I pretend to be sad. Then I forget about it. Sometimes I talk to myself thinking that only stars can hear me, but I get responses from people. I have to reply to them, i.e., conceal the true motives that got me talking. Sometimes I tell them about a tree, a cherry-tree that used to grow in my back yard, covering the roof of the house with its branches, under which I used to hide in the spring and early summer while skipping school. The preponderance of the dead over the living forces one to believe in the inevitable encounter—otherwise, it's hard to understand what determines the consistency of this imbalance. And yes, the silk curtains with oak-leaf embroidery, which used to hang on the bookcase, were also of unequal length. There will be evening tomorrow. Today there was one already. The imbalance of the world is the nature of the mirror.

I must note that occasionally I experienced considerable inconveniences. But how great really was *this very* desire? And were the inconveniences really that bad? These questions seem difficult to answer.

I repeat, everything mentioned above—and much else—happened invisibly for me, and memory never dragged me into the mirror labyrinths of comparison. No prophecies. I have to confess, at first, the taste of analogy was strange... Later I realized that this taste could mean the absence of the taste of defeat. And frankly, I had dreamed constantly of the latter ever since I got sick of the rarefied "shining" of endless victory. A train rolled by. The gate of autumn. A gleam of light encased in the frozen air. To take a step or two—to the frail branch that can't bear the wind's crushing mass. Further away from the whisper is the quiet cold in the clarity of awakening. The cry of a bird, the sinuous banner of smoke. Fingers, sticky with sweat, destroy the altruistic illusion of keyboard labor. Every touch requires completion. Even if it's a punctual click. Completion as the only measure of one's spinning around. A question: what will the moon see when it stops raining, when the train is gone, when the gate of autumn is shut? The letter closes with a trivial phrase: "only a gaze catching up with a departing gaze—such is vision that leads to what we know as things." I don't like it. I hate the weather, faces, shreds of phrases to which I am doomed. A few wasted things, speech shattered like a muddy country road—will the moon see itself at dawn in these parts? Thin diagonals of the landscape are attractive.

My boss often reproaches me for neglecting common (?) rules. According to her, without them—no matter what sort of illuminations we are blessed with (indeed, who are "we"?)—we (we again!) wouldn't even earn ourselves a cup of tea.

Terre arable du songe! Qui parle de batir? — J'ai vu la terre distribuée en de vastes espaces et ma pensée n'est point distraite du navigateur, read the screen saver. I use someone else's computer. As well as someone else's money, words, and dreams. Will my death be as alien as my life? It has to be this way. In such cases I'm usually silent. Nothing to talk about. In other cases too. Declarations of love are exercises in the use of metaphors. An approach is endless, like a fall in the illusory wheels of galaxies. Strange, but I have no one to argue with! Indeed, it has to be this way. I'm even prepared to assume there is no reason to argue. But everyone must hurry—ankle-deep in water, under the vaults of black trees with heavy leaves—hurry because night is coming to make him who hurries even uglier. I forget why I started talking about all… this. I must immediately do an inventory of all events that had me enter them in the log of the real. It seems to have rained since morning when I got to the office—it rained all the time, and later. Then we counted days by apples. Also adjectival changes in every plot line. I made coffee, sank into an armchair by the grimy Zenith while behind the window, in the cul-de-sac, it kept pouring down—I was only separated from the rain by glass and white Venetian blinds. It was then that the phone rang, he thinks. And no one bothered to answer. Coffee's ready. Sure. The machine picked up. Never leave any messages for anyone. All messages are fog falling out in sleet on roofs, pavements, and objects. Voice, fog, indeterminacy—sometimes, just cruelty. What kind of cruelty, one may ask? To whom should I complain? To whom should I address my written statement? I really don't know—it's customary to say this; one says what's customary. Here is a tree. Is it a tree? No, it's a map of Petersburg.

"[...] wake up if you're there! You're not? Then listen. I don't know much about that subject. It would probably take a long investigation. As far as the cult itself, I'm not quite sure which one you mean. I know little about it—only that they worship the spirit of Gurdjieff, and that their compound is a couple of hours' drive from San Jose. There could be up to two thousand of them—some live there permanently, others come and go. I haven't yet found out what they do—as I said, it would take time—I'm only worried they'd try to convert me if I came close. Remember that story with the Mormons? At first I thought you were asking about David Koresh, but he burnt down—literally, after the FBI cracked down on him with tanks. Another horrible story. Koresh himself (accent on the last syllable!) was in the business of unsealing David's seven seals. He almost unsealed them all, but someone tipped the police that his people collected guns in their bunker. That they did—quite legally in fact—but the rumor was they were reassembling guns into something automatic. Instead of tracking him down and arresting him outside the bunker, the FBI waited till Sunday, when all 80 people including women and children sat there busy with their seals, surrounded them with tanks and helicopters and told them to get out one by one. Then they started to unseal them. The cult people shot back, it lasted a week; then they drilled holes and started to gas them—that's how everything went up in flames. Perhaps Koresh and his buddies lit it up—or perhaps they didn't—in any event, they all burnt to death; only about ten people survived, they're now on trial, as are the FBI for their criminal misunderstanding of the essence of cults. I think the FBI (together with the FTA who actually performed the operation) proved to be complete assholes who just wanted to drive around in tanks and shoot at stuff—a horrible tragedy in the end. Anyway, gotta go, back to my mines, digging coal for a victory over capitalism. Don't call me till Monday—I'll be in Palo Alto. There are complications at our branch there. Another strange story. I'll tell you later."

They hang up the phone at the other end. At this end, they were having fun. I'm not sure the other party was equally amused. An old man on a bicycle with a sack on his back was laughing his head off. She began to appear in my dreams. I dreamed I was at some conference in New Jersey or Wisconsin. I've come to my hotel room to change—my clothes, wet and sticky from the heat, cling to my body like Deianira's gown. I have to peel them off like rubber glue with tightly wrapped insects asleep in its egypt, slowly and steadily sleepwalking to the heart; she's already emerging from the shower, and what's really important—I'm sure of it now—is that she's the sister of the one whom I must, by all means, remember—whose name is drilled into my brain by thawing chrysalises; the name promises to shine some day in the image of a disconnected, stray letter, empty and fragile like the chitin growth of hope, and I'm only guessing her features in her sister's; the window offers a very different view—looks like Kamenets-Podolsky—but it's impossible to put it all together into something indeterminate, there is only that which there is. So hard to get rid of these clothes. There is nothing underneath her long gown, only white socks. She sits down on the edge of the bed and, spreading her legs, leans forward to pull up a sock. I am convinced that she habitually renders judgements and, moreover, recollections, mesmerizingly unnecessary, but many will have to pay for her. Wet hair is the only remnant of the dream. The rest is fiction. But I need a face that hasn't found its indeterminacy within the limits of the journey.

I liked my boss (fem.)... The appearance of the laughing old man on a bicycle forces one to remember the hierarchy of Tarot cards. She is elegant, has good connections. Sometimes we comfort ourselves on her desk where no single sheet of paper is to be found. When she steps into her skirt, thrown on the floor, and leans slightly forward, as though about to step into a swimming pool or to pull up a sock, she resembles Fanny Ardant. Then I'm embarrassed again by my dirty fingernails. And I lie once more, promising myself never to bite them again. A minute later I forget about our relationship, knowing that her memory of it (of me) won't last much longer either—and thus till evening, when stepping out of the shower she'll suggest "let's-have-a-drink-it's-been-a-long-day". WIND CHIMES. And her shrewdness is undeniable. But above all, her style of dress. Possibly, she has other qualities as well, but my guess is, they are far less valuable than the ones just mentioned. What's her name; the phone rings; it's probably Karl; I don't think he'll have much time for conversation. The fact of a third cup of coffee; of a cigarette; a few phrases; a semicolon. The pliability of computer keys is entrancing. The reality of tireless erasure. Fr. Lob doesn't think so. His head is propped on his hand: crossing his eyes toward the moving lips (it's been a hard day), he is reading:

"The spot where the old woman coincided with the car was empty. The sky was overcast with a whitish shroud. Everything became diffuse and boring. Dikikh looked down (was he interested in traces? I wonder who called...), shrugged his shoulders: a face was looking at him from a first-floor window—it was either that of a child or of someone ageless. Smash the jar. Set the birds and worms free. A chessboard was in front of the creature. White had a positional advantage. A raindrop fell on a black square. The child (or the freak) was unshaven. (To whom shall be left the hairless face of a midget?) A word always transports one into the unbraiding of writing that has neither a place for a word, nor for the very definition of "a word" in its locks. The freak was silent. It was the silence of the earth embarrassed by a distortion in the correlation of sounds. They and I are driven by composition, narrative—a hope of acquisition. And besides, the rain has been falling so unbearably long, multiplying itself in the boom of the well. Narrative is perhaps one of the conditions of a story's unfolding, i.e., of the emergence of a knot which is both the connections and their "focal point".

"Do you play with every passer-by?" asked Dikikh, squinting theatrically. "For money?" He felt in his jacket for cigarettes, found the pack in the inside pocket and fiddled with it. "My dear man, playing for money is wrong."

There are three suns in the sky. Too few. But we'll wait for ten. We just need to be patient. No need to hurry.

Some of us remember months of lingering, painful rain and nights that seemed three times nocturnal. Extinct lights were kept at the bottom of vision, like irregular-shaped stones. Try to take them off. Besides, wet leaves, so many of them—or so few—who needs them? Parched fabric of hearing, silicon dust, gardens embroidering the chromed slopes of nicotine sleeplessness. There the fog barely moves moments not woven by space—they existed but, it seems, before their "birth", and the rest, including the stretched shadows of what was once called fear, is of the order of the insignificant. But what never existed for you was, from the very beginning, lost from your sight, from your vocabulary and syntax, as though someone else's muttering was heard behind your usual figures of speech, making it hard for you to come back to what you already said. Like fish and weeds, like eyelids, pupils, like lines—further, you see him walking under the vaults of trees, their black tops are woven together. Every line, every word, every sign, appearing in the focus of nothingness (knot), submerge in limbo, like the purest ashes. Isn't this what you've been looking for? On some magnification, doors fly open, clocks strike, nobody and nothing appears. Is it not surprising that you celebrate New Year all your life? We thought it would only happen once, at the end of October, when gulf winds bring sleet, and birds keep standing in the wind, rising higher and higher, motionless and idle like angels. Anticipating this moment, we thought it would never come. We were lied to. It's useless to burn watch fires and papers; more useless even, to collect black flakes in the hope of a literal resurrection. First, the contour disintegrates into a broken line, then into a row of points. Their relentless ocular tracing no longer yields the illusion of continuity; space also disappears—a point is silent and punctual, just as it is discontinuous in its lack of origin.

"Those who want to, play," nodded the child. "Those who want to, lose. But frankly, few people walk by here. They mostly drive."

"And you? Are you always here?"

"What do you mean 'always'? I was born here. What about you?"

"I was born there..." Dikikh waved behind his shoulder. "In Washington."

The face of the infant bent over the chessmen was full of unseen inspiration.

"It's a neighborhood on Vasilyevsky Island. All wooden houses," Dikikh explained and cleared his throat. "Barracks, houses of weatherboard. Washington, in short."

"No," said the child after some thinking. "Never been there."

Then he moved a white pawn. Dikikh glanced at the board.

"And where *have* you been?"

"To very few places, really," said the freak and shoved the black queen forward.

"That's bad," uttered Dikikh. "A hasty move. The knight is being threatened. You need to get away."

"I can't get very far. Got no legs. Lost them a long time ago." The first-floor resident rubbed his unshaven chin. "But my arms are remarkably strong. Once, when I was run over by a car, I lifted it up with my hands. So as not to perish."

"Why are you telling me this?" asked Dikikh. "OK, look... Very good, let's move our bishop over there, Mr. Procrustes"

"What Procrustes?" said the old woman, her eyes still on the board. "What on earth do you mean?" A drop fell on the board, on a black square. The drop slowly turned into dust. The square became a prism.

"He also earned his living on the road. Like yourself."

"What sort of a traveler are you then? You've got a car, a revolver, women, bodyguards, a cell phone, and music."

"Nothing of the kind. I get around by motorboat. Have been for ages," said Dikikh.

"Such a pity."

"What is it now?" Dikikh looked up.

"Dunno. Actually, an old woman was run over here an hour ago. It's her I pity. I close my eyes and imagine how she walked—poor thing, must have lost all she had in life, her best years, love, taste for adventure—how she walked thinking about her children, not just thinking but praying for their souls..."

"Wait," Dikikh blurted out, "what children? She was an old woman, wasn't she?"

"Why can't an elderly woman have children if she had everything in life?"

"Hasn't she lost it all?"

"Well, the children must have remained. Such was her fate."

Now it was quite apparent that the creature wasn't a freak at all, but a lovely child in a blue cambric shirt, his hair streaked with pure gold.

"Right across from here. Smashed to smithereens," continued the child. "Hey, look, it's pouring down now. On our street you sometimes pity everything. What a bummer."

Still looking at the board, the half-child, half-freak pointed at Dikikh's stomach. Dikikh mechanically drew it in, looked around, threw up his head. The rain turned to drizzle. It got long and boring.

"You wouldn't believe me, but I'm actually happy for such circumstances," continued the toothless chess player from his first-floor window. "That's a nasty move with your bishop there! For a second I thought you meant to hurt me with your Procrustes... Me being legless and all... I read something about Procrustes. Ah, you shouldn't have given up that pawn."

Dikikh didn't hear that. He'd turned around sharply and walked away down Kirpichny Lane, toward the Aeroflot booking office, to get to the bridge by the Spit where his motorboat was waiting and where up ahead, on the right, there was a guttering, candy-wrapped angel holding a sweet trumpet. Dikikh was wearing a mustard-colored corduroy jacket. He had changed his shirt after dinner for a dark, silk one. The description of clothes is one of the most important requirements for sustaining the intensity of intrigue. Sometimes it serves as retardation.

"Wait! Where are you going?" he heard someone yell behind him. "You won! Don't go!"

Dikikh stopped, not understanding what was being said. Immediately, he wanted to write a letter in which, without beating around the bush, he'd consistently relate his version: Ivan Petrovich comes to the window and realizes that now he knows why he is so inexpressibly depressed every morning. Vera is right, thinks Piotr Ivanovich, he is really old and can no longer give her anything in life. One needs to face the truth. And Sergei Mikhailovich also thinks that everything passes—his love for Vera, for the children, for his life's cause... This sweeping emotion gently pushes him down on his knees and makes him kiss the balcony step.

When Dikikh was turning around to face the voice, he managed to dodge a fifty-kopeck coin headed relentlessly for his eyebrow.

"You never said a word again." A line from some old romantic song. I began to lose you. I was killing you slowly, with indescribable pleasure. What was the reason for my groundless worrying? Mandatory euonymus shrubs. Sometimes I did it in front of witnesses. They remained mute in the collectivized vision that never became pure pleasure. Later I had the unusual urge to write a letter to E. I went through the letter drawer to refresh my memory—her note was mentioned above—but found nothing. No one ever cleans our place. Soon we'll be buried under heaps of empty coffee boxes, beer cans, papers, and other garbage. Garbage is as unavoidable as good paintings. It's much harder to explain the composition of garbage than it is to answer the question of what memory's fabric consists of, or which party is going to win the next election.

What happened to me usually remained an impenetrable conjunction of coincidences within which even a keener mind would hardly recognize a pattern. Very early in life—I think at about 12—I'd already come to a clear conclusion. I remember the moment well. My parents decided to take me to Moscow. The boy was to look at the beautiful heart of the Motherland, or at least to press his ear to it and listen to the great country's rhythm. He had done enough loafing about with all sorts of street bums and girls, pigeons and fights—enough floating through the city's beaches and squares, enough reflecting in the ancient waters of provincial living. Childhood is also a province. The city resembled a game; its rules were self-determination. The rest is a return; its trajectory spreads much farther than the point of imaginary coincidence.

The trip was something of a gift for my school vacation, even though my quarter results were poor as could be and the teachers' council had a few times threatened me with expulsion. My transgressions were countless; they included frequent fights in which I, for various reasons, was forced to participate, invariably disgusted by my own fear. I constantly had blood gushing down my face—the knot of a wire brace mounted on my two front teeth stuck out and if I made the slightest error, i.e., if I ever failed to dodge a blow in time, the opponent's fist would naturally hit me right in the jaw; the knotted wire would strike my lip, which naturally would make me furious, and as a result, I'd "come down hard" on the enemy, who would be surprised by the sudden turn in the battle. The disgusting brace was something like the sword of Demosthenes. Its sting hidden in my mouth was turned, alas, against myself, and even the slightest miscalculation was immediately and mercilessly punished. Silent and gentle, we tasted the bliss of apprenticeship in the shadow of plane trees. The garrote, i.e., brace, was installed in September and by March I already forgot what it meant to take a punch. It was quite fortunate because my head doesn't take punches well—when hit, I immediately want to lie down, open a book, take a nap; I feel an incredible sweetness in my stomach, and the coziness that rolls in from all around is simply irresistible. Shnift, by contrast, was of a very different breed. One could have taken him for a Kshatriya, were he not of the Brahman varna. It might even have seemed that he flaunted his remarkable ability. It obviously fooled his enemies, of whom there were many—he gambled, which is not an easy sport; one needs to know things in order to win or sometimes just to break even, and most important of all, to clear out before it's too late. But since he gambled, he "knew" people, he knew that people had a penchant for petty, cowardly revenge; he knew that those who sat down to play with him (usually two of them as the game took three) expected him to play the part of a brainless sucker; additionally Shnift had a very sharp eye, shaved fingers, and enough madness in the head to feel not just his own cards but also other players'; but then these cards also had to be thought through in order to figure out the situation, which took several hours, though scheming wasn't what mattered—he'd win all the same even though he drank as much as the rest—what mattered was that when, two or three days later, it was time for the losers to pay up (as mentioned, there were sometimes two of them) and when they, as could be expected, got worked up and acted pugnacious—while he, mind you, already had their money in the hand—after all, part of the skill was to make a convincing argument (indeed, nobody played for matches, sooner or later you had to hold in the hand what was rightfully yours)—then it would turn out *they* were the suckers, a fact they obviously didn't like a bit; then they'd realize that everything was nothing but trouble, that they'd been singled out and fucked over, with no tricks—they were simply allowed to go with the flow, heading where they wanted to go—it was at that moment that they'd start waving their arms, they'd fling them around, but Shnift would just stand there unperturbed, stuffing the money in his shirt, with his head jerking back and forth—he could stand there that way as long as was necessary—his eyes, too, were in place, though red from sleepless nights and booze; but then he'd wake up and switch on, and it was good to see him lean forward slightly and start the thrashing. I remember Lasutra and I witnessed such an episode once: Shnift, his right hand still preoccupied with the money, was already bashing the guy's head with his left. He knew very well whom to do first—"the cheekiest one"—he did just that, starting with that very person who immediately lost all courage and walked away as though asleep. The Night of the Zombies, that sort of stuff!—but Shnift let him take a few steps, then turned completely around and hit him in the head yet again, this time from the side and with some strangely curious look on his face, as if aiming further, for his dreams, while we watched blood drip from his ear. It formed a black clot on his red shirt. At that time everyone wore dyed red shirts and green pants with wide cuffs. At that time everyone sang "I love you, life!" A summer shower started a minute later. Everyone's hair got wet and stuck together. Meanwhile, Shnift jumped aside, hopped to a hole in the fence and was gone. We fought with whatever came in handy—bicycle chains, pumps, lead-cast shock-absorbers, jumpers... Sometimes with our bare hands—but not very often. Those who didn't gamble had no money and only dreamed of sex (sometimes, during morning classes, they'd get erections and refuse to come to the blackboard), yet even then, there was already quite enough violence to lose any taste for it. I haven't been there for ages. At one time I heard that Shnift had been axed to death by his best friend Krol—axed at a corner, by the entrance to Savoy. It happened a year after Pakutsa was knifed on Pirogovskaya. Perhaps everything happened differently, I don't know. At my age I easily mix up my own memories with other people's dreams. This is how we lived this life. First one of its parts, then another. We've become a stilted simile.

It all happened this way, but entirely differently. A garden at night, silhouettes of people at a table, an enormous cherry-tree in sparse, floating clouds of light from an old lamp at the table's edge. I am moving fragments of the testimony to a different center of gravity. Lurching over and keeping the balance in my participial shell—yet quite differently.

"I feel unbearably confused. The garden is enormous. The book is closed, and the bird falls like a stone into the focus of my admiration of history. But this isn't enough. My embarrassment also comes from something else: from the silence in the souls of madmen. In their eyes the garden is enormous, yet they're limitless before its greatness. My thoughts are like a military orchestra; they're so quiet they'd never meet words. But is the word really so unavoidable? Does a thought seek a word—or its essence, dreams fragmented by a manifold, drawn by an inexplicable desire to their own origin and passing through the latter as doomed deities treading on sand, losing their nature when they touch sand's every fraction? Is the word really as inescapable as the movement of sand fragments?"

"I know that madmen are usually quiet because mirrors for them are only a cause for curiosity and subsequent insincere despair. Hence they prefer dark boats that leak resin in the heat. I know: a cause for curiosity and despair. Like ancient ships, they're sown out of all the dead people's fingernails, out of all the read books buried in the air like water, the pages of which are cold and transparent. Do they look for the word? Sometimes they touch their faces and scream, but the scream only annoys those around them. The scales of choosing between this and that."

"But the silence traveling in the souls of the unborn resembles drops that never reach the bowl of time. What encounters its own image in this silence? Dark boats and repetitions? What is it filled with? With its 'never' and 'nowhere' finding their own reflections? Does 'time' know 'never'? This contradiction is fragile because, according to the manufacturer's warranty, the device shall meet the State Standards Commission specifications #16617-87, if used, transported, and stored under proper conditions."

"I know that time is hot, wide, wet leaves applied to ailing heads; it is leaves used to wrap flaming foreheads and to cool off temples. I know that the rated voltage = B. The human head has so many parts—so many segments, semi-circles, proud lines, and hot, wet leaves!"

"Such boats are usually made of tree-bark sheens and sheens of lead, but the echo can't assimilate itself; 'cold and transparent' can't realize itself in a noun, remaining a lost indication. The squeaking of stones underfoot—that's more like it. Silky ribbons everywhere you look. But you can't discount fog, as well as overall dimensions and the control band…"

"Or take for example, screams of children who easily overtake the birds in the autumn sky. Many of them are pensive, their hair is long, their eyes are green. But some of them are famous for adding letters to insignificant objects and phenomena. Their appearance in the ceremonies of future-telling often entails lies because they aren't really children. Nor are their life signs stable."

"As far as I understand, these creatures belong to no one—in the sense that I understand 'belonging'."

"Grammatically—yes; they do indeed presuppose the illusions of tautology. But this isn't meant for us…"

"The land at the very center of ether is equally silent. How does one get there? How does one reach its shores? Is it for us to achieve? Can we really do it? What's the technology of connecting muscular effort to image? Metal to acids?"

"Doubtless, all this is known to those who sail burning waters in heavy nocturnal boats, to those who understand that a thermometer probe is susceptible to the impact of cold streams. Wrapped in wide cloaks, they contemplate their own reflections joyously burning in the ashes of the flame."

"But it can't go on like this."

"No, it won't. It isn't fatigue, but exhaustion. Its continuation is doubtful. This is why they count among their brothers fragile formulae of extended vision and electrons with strong nocturnal positions. Their sisters are irreproachable as they possess empires of comparisons. Their every confession starts with a negation. Their love is slow, like lip-covered eyes."

"It's now becoming more obvious why no knowledge can contain either an electron or a tree—both, and particularly the latter, can't be reduced to a result. Let's take any tree at hand. Let's call it bougainvillea."

"No, poplar. Or a cut in the connecting cord."

"See, you're still the same. No matter what name you pronounce, the tree won't become you, and you won't become the tree. There'll always be two of you. Furthermore, each will have its own light and darks sides. Like money mistaken for books, for example. This is why you started with the silence of madmen. But ignorance can't contain the tree either—it's too small to find itself in ignorance. Nor can ignorance contain you."

"God resembles all of this taken together. All this is so, but in an entirely different way."

"Yes. He looks like a pronoun and all letters at once. I'd like to see them unwittingly erased from the blackboard (a proper name...). He also resembles madmen who don't know why they have mirrors, rusty radiators, wire flowers, and plaster snails displayed in front of them."

"And finally, Kondraty Savelyevich, are we going carp-fishing on Sunday? Does our agreement still stand?"

"I'd like to know who'll finally get around to fixing the boat," adds grandfather enthusiastically.

"God resembled sleepless sleep," mother quietly continues her story. She is wiping cups. And the light in her hair is the same light that ascends through cherry-tree branches.

"He resembles the love in which there is no trace of love, love whose thread escapes scissors; He resembles your birth from which you are forever withdrawn. What's written there? Whose handwriting is it? Like a black flag torn down by wind and rain. Flying into the night. No, this is from another source. And inside the body—wouldn't you know—there's nothing. Nothing but boom. Do you remember the bloom of boom?"

"What's written there is different. It says *Operating Manual*."

"Then what am I for?"

6 April, 1939

What I mean (and it concerns that same book on viruses) is that the character (his/her gaze) broke the love connection with someone by the name 404. While surfing the net, you learn that "Error 404" is the message telling you that a file or web site isn't found on a server. I think you were accurate about the psychotic style of the chase, pursuit, or search I'm thinking of. A multitude of other voices tells me that this is exactly how matters stand. Today mother was fired from her job for some error. She misplaced something... It must have been some object. I don't remember what exactly. Thus, a "gaze" (which is always the gaze of the reader, unknown to him- or herself to the very end) wanders around web sites, deep in its contemplation of life and its love of Error 404.

15 January, 1948

You're right, I saw those pages: they were flashbacks to love—a madness of a kind that doesn't let go of our poor character. It resembles flashing, burning stars and galaxies that make the word *distance* laughable. On the other hand, one could surmise that 404 infected our character's body with a certain virus (dimension?), even though he/she/it wasn't entirely certain of it. Our character learned about this fact from another person in the play, "SD" (Supplementary Document) who, at the time, was psychoanalyst to other characters... Yet SD could also have been the source of the virus. In other words, it is quite obvious that we have much more paranoia than necessary here. But I insist on their visual materialization, on their real presence. Write to me at the following address: D137: bff404fl.

August, 1952

I am only interested in the idea of the gaze because the gaze (or vision) is the only real thing penetrating cyberspace and the net. "Ontologically" speaking, I imagine the nameless vision of the reader, exfoliating from him/her and living its own life. But does it see what can be seen—for example, its own self? Finally, we're coming to the conclusion that the reader needs refuge where the narrative, which we began with, can emerge. Such refuge can be found only in the literal body of the reader—reader of his own history. Vision is fully consumed by this body.

Thus, what sort of information does vision possess?

I like your idea of the net as a theater. It's definitely a theatrical mode of being—i.e., one ruled by the laws of theater. It's a show moving (and cutting) across space and time [what sort of space? There's only something remotely resembling "Bergsonian" time]. Who said so? I did. Well, yes, of course, I won't argue. But if we use transgression, then we must also use the most important theatrical transgression. And in some strange way, we will see what is seen by our gaze. The type of vision produced by theater...

Yes, you asked me if I'd seen her. Sometimes I think it was her, but she didn't want to be recognized. I'm not particularly certain of this, and I limit myself to arbitrary conclusions.

"And what happens next?" asked Turetsky.

"Nothing," answered Fr. Lob. "That's the end of the notebook."

"It's impossible!"

"What's impossible?"

"It's impossible that he was writing like this at the time!"

"Yes, he was," said Fr. Lob. "Anything's possible. This is exactly how he wrote in those years. Of course, his style changed radically much later."

"What do you mean 'much later'?"

"Well..." Fr. Lob stirred his fingers in the air. "After some time."

"Bergsonian? But something else is interesting:

who said it?"

"Maybe I did. But frankly, I already don't remember."

Bewilderment will be a lasting reminder of itself. Days of bewilderment, when suddenly everything is like nothing else in the world. I'm asking you, what do you pity? OK, I agree. It was then that I imagined she had died. We were lying side by side. Behind the walls of the shed, the noon was blazing yellow; an imaginary sun pulsated under my eyelids, and her hot hand was resting on my thigh.

"Why are you crying?" she asked.

"Because you died," I replied.

"Well then, what was left after my death? And what am I for? You've answered none of my questions."

Yes, but I expected a shadow would flit by the window. The shadow flitted by a window that had nothing to do with me. Now I/he/she/they were dead, or rather we both were dead because we were flying under my eyelids to the imaginary sun carrying off the romantic fragments of the closed book and the enormous garden—also part of the narrative. They were departing into the excessively deep layers of diminishing. Such are the optics. Such are danger, homeland, circle.

Anyway, I was standing on the train platform and, sinking into the languor of the hypnotic state into which I was pulled by the monotonous spiral of legitimately repeating one and the same thing (a monotony that completely erases the possibility of distinctions). Suddenly I saw an inscription on the embankment slope. Birds were pecking my eyes. The eyes were far from sharp. Neither birds, nor eyes, nor the rest of the people (neuter gender).

You're right, I've never been a child. The inscription I saw was common for those times—it was laid out in large chunks of white-washed road metal. In his fairy tales, the boy marked the journey with white pebbles. Speed overpowers discontinuity: the role of various mythologies. The blurred white spots (today my myopia is even worse) read (I don't remember) either "*until we meet again*" or "*beware of the gantry crane*", and then all was lost, though I think that a search for the true inscription would have led me to the handy (you must take my age into account!) maxim regarding truth or its opposite. The causality of heavenly mechanics: thunder succeeds lightning. Acoustic presence is inherited from its already expired visual counterpart. It seems we were obsessed with reading lightning. Thunder presented redundant and slow excess. Asking a question, I already know your answer. The impossibility of a reverse perspective. To this day the banality of youthful discoveries fails to repel me; it only causes a habitually acerbic feeling of detached sadness. But other anticipations of that time, awkwardly translated into a rigorously mastered language—weren't they in equal degree unavoidably ridiculous? Not at all. Perhaps the words "truth" and "lie" were used to set up a dichotomy not because people were unwilling to establish their meanings but because these words were in turn conventional figures, concealing entirely different prerequisites of things and connections, or at least of their dimension. Such a reading may have been the result of a visual aberration, or of the arbitrary angle at which stones gleamed before the eyes of a boy on a train, who in an unimaginably remote future would need this very episode—in which vision comes to the boil on the edges of substance and disintegrates in the whiteness of hissing granules—he would need it to accumulate time, or to bring into the narrative an invisible moment of chance and to separate himself from the fiction of what he's describing, i.e., the authentic. The effect of stereoscopy, the emasculation of habitual bifurcation: everything takes place before the moment unfolds. Time is redundant.

This is exactly what I said to a man who stopped by my window on a rainy summer day. What could I offer him? A game of chess? One or two curious observations? I still don't know who was passing by or where I read about it. It wasn't the phrase itself that mattered, nor the fact that someone had disappeared without a trace, though we'll have to talk about this too—but to every thing there is a season, even the reading of lightning. One could stop here, on the bridge, above the buildings, and look down below, to a place where a river used to flow once. One could open a bottle of beer, then smoke a cigarette—there's mother-land for you. It turns out you don't pity any of this. Neither the river, nor the bridges, nor autumn floods. And it's simple. You just need to be certain of one thing: that they won't cut off both your arms as a sign of unrequited love for your nation, even though there are thousands of such nations, and it's not all that clear which of them considers you their inalienable property. It depends. Then you won't make do with mere detachment and sadness—you'll have to learn writing with your teeth. What's there to pity? With nails on glass. With water on sand. Fine. And when you realize that this too is useless, when you grasp that the world is an ordinary agglomerate of possibilities, in which greatness and nothingness have the indisputable right—a right with no need for guarantees—to appear at one and the same moment, and that both greatness and nothingness are the very namelessness of the moment's disappearance, perhaps then it will be time to realize that there's nothing worth writing about. But nobody's writing. To take word after word, in a deliberately slow movement, to the end of the sentence, to a collapse, to a brilliant, infinitesimal flash. A flash so intangible that the heart stops in a strange joy, and even the mind is hardly able to find its match in any possible repetition—none of these repetitions (including imaginary ones) would be able to grasp its exploding dispersal, when nothing appears in the place of the anticipated emergence, when something like suspended speculative dust takes an endlessly long time to fall out on objects, anticipations, things, and memories—on the one hand, preserving them, rendering them eternally invulnerable, and on the other, altering their outlines perhaps by the very quality of inevitable permanence in the incompleteness of expected transformation. Only morning dust discovers the path of the ray. We wake up. The world enchants us. You ask the world, "Do you remember your night?" There is no answer. The fence remains unpainted. But it's even more beautiful to contemplate a ray dispersed in the pupils of our eyes—a ray that brings, like the galaxies of dreams, something that failed to become a thing of existence.

Still, frankly speaking, one had to make a certain effort. No matter how you hid it, this effort would sooner or later be revealed. For many years I observed—not without fascination—my process of growing into what habitually comprises the plan of this life, gradually discovering, or rather, developing an ornament that had only to do with me (incidentally, I have little belief in such a relation). It's as difficult to describe life's components as it is to describe the composition of any given thing, its projections, shadows, and time. I still can't manage the task too well. One probably ought to speak of salvation. But even as I pronounce this word, I unfortunately imagine nothing and, as it were, fall into a painful, expectant silence. If at this moment I declared I love devouring my own and other people's feces, I am positive others would sigh with relief. It would be clear that what I write is literature and doesn't claim to be anything else. Except perhaps, the "mystery of Being". But how happy

I'd be just to write literature, to talk about my cherished plans, to joyfully hover, allowing myself thoughtful discourse on the return of sentimentality to writing, on the significance of angels, on infants, electronic webs, and holy fools—all this with a certain particular facial expression. Too many exclamation points. It's understandable. Too many words. Indeed. Instead, I'm too consumed by narcissism, too busy measuring my headache with metal compasses. Sometimes I think I still know a place where one doesn't feel sick of people's presence, but I also know that I'd sooner see the back of my head than find that place. There are other places, though. Sometimes I return from them a complete idiot, and only God knows how much effort it takes me to prolong that state every time. Some women (who remind me of myself) occasionally, in an outburst of passion (disgust?) or sincerity tell me I remind them of a Levantine Greek. I ask her where she saw a Levantine Greek. In some picture, she says (in a flash, my imagination draws one of those pictures covered with the hoarfrost of flimsy paper, with their yellowed, sugary corners half-broken), in college. I try to imagine what a college is; frankly, I fail. Failure after failure. Life is life. Then I dream of a sfumato picture—someone in wide pants, with a Ukrainian top-knot on his shaved head, with a lyre on his back and a rein coiled around his fist, uttering distinctly, "we inherited the cosmos of Levantine Greeks, but after reflection and graduated (?) wars, the cosmos underwent significant changes: now it's weak, worm-infested and needs something it can't acknowledge because of its own feebleness, which it values above the ability it previously held to freeze into an impenetrable fire crystal in the anticipation of spring tide. God abandons man only for man to learn about His absence. But in the unstoppable time of abandonment, man grasps the absence of God as the phenomenon of His presence in His disappearance. No possible image can reflect this absence where you comprehend possibility, destiny, and the failure of both. Let's take another example. They talk of 'nearing death'. The growth of death evidently follows from the notion of an unflinching shrinking of life, of its waning, thinning, fading in the desire to be replaced by its opposite. Yet at the moment of death, life is fulfilled as its own complete cessation, flawless in the fullness of its passion and presence."

The Greek on the can slowly lowers his left eyelid, and I closely dodge a sequin headed for my forehead. Pain thaws out again in the vision dissected by a line on the one side of which we are, while on the other, we're no more, never have been, never will be, and where the only existing thing is the possibility of being in each of the three tenses. This one thing is divisible in two. One part belongs to me, and the other to the Greek, or to her who is telling me about him as she sits on the bed in a terry gown and white socks, successfully impersonating her own sister.

But there isn't a shade of animosity in our relationship. Stars grow dim, the eastern horizon lightens up. Rains fall. Another war is over. Because what happens is a secret deliberation of the necessary forces, and we're left here to testify about it in the future. But you, she says with a tinge of surprise (or rather, the surprise is imagined by the reader of this sentence), you're beyond what I'd call justice. Yes, I reply to her then, I agree— perhaps because it isn't quite clear to me what you mean. And besides, how can you talk about justice when ever since morning the same cards are dealt to us, when sleet keeps falling for a second day in a row, if landscapes fall into poverty, if there is no money—if every now and then you find in your hands the same photograph of a Greek standing in the street at night with a pizza slice in his hand, when the upper stories of buildings murkily smolder in crimson glow, and the translucent lucerne spilled down below is about to change into the twilight of smoky amethyst, as usually happens here, at the corner of Mokhovaya and Pestel, where you feel your brain becoming again a deserted focus of all the streets in the world and where everything around you seems so real that you feel an unbearable urge to wake up? But you always have to walk one street only, no matter which side you choose. Or which destination.

It would be fair to assume that in our youth an expansion of precisely this kind seemed the only alternative to something a vague awareness of which we carry within ourselves long before it separates into *this* and *that*. Drop by drop, the moon flowed into the mica ruptures of seconds. The juice of henbane, goose-foot under the scythe, the mutter of rowing—the colorless glow of the gullet and the hair of haze on the wind's glass crest. Do we know that *we know*, do we know how each of us knows it, and then, thereafter, later, when, as though wandering in the gardens of synonyms, walking down the staircase, step after step, overlooking the absence of underfoot support with surprising ease (heather, the barely audible splashes and crunch of frost-bitten sand that today signify a thin ring on the fourth finger—another detail leading from the signifier to synaesthesia), do we know *what each of us* signifies for the knowledge in his possession? A warm strike of the wind diffused all debates. A collision with a branch, rain, metal, and ashes. I passed here many times. It's important to understand the process of lexical selection. The choice of a word is an act of consciousness that creates a reality to which, for the lack of anything else, I am pulled by the stream—yet one can never land on these strange shores. A redistribution of meanings, a liberation of senses: a copper-framed magnifying glass, a mock-up frigate, a book opened at a page where the corner of one's eye can cursorily excise: "There is a tree somewhere from which sticks are excised; these sticks are quite beautiful; their motley colors are reminiscent of tiger skin. The tree is heavy: if you threw it on firm ground, it would break like clay"; a little further away, behind the cut glass of the cupboard, a four-inch-high marble egg, a whisk of faded, once painted feathers, an amber fish, with a bifurcated spinal fin embedded in the fake crystal of a strange device for measuring the heights of all possible moons at once. We give preference to some words (which, god knows for what reason, are extracted from the catalogs of non-being—i.e., myself), other words remain their mere contours, a prayer of enumeration, emerging in consciousness as a vain aspiration to join the thing that parted a long time ago with the blissful moment of object-less-ness in its claim on being. Return is impossible. Same cards are dealt to us for days on end. The passageway from Liteiny to Mayakovsky St. is now blocked. Don't forget. Actually, there's never been a passage there. A familiar mistake. Look for another street. For other windows and voices.

And on the night between Wednesday and Friday, Dikikh had a dream. Whistling a tune, he walks on something like a roof or meadow—a flat surface, anyhow—and sees stars splashing underfoot. "Holes," thinks Dikikh, and he is right, because he is indeed walking on a meadow, and the light is blinding. This happens when the sky is overcast with a glowing, milky haze; it's unbearably bright by noon. The light emerges from nowhere and extends no further than its limits; only heavy, slumbering weeds stretch out to infinity. In the morning, when there's obviously no dew and all signs point to impending rain, not a drop falls, and the outlines of objects—not even outlines proper, but something in the eye's pupil, something that meets the purple-yellow glow of the traces left by a thing in the wake of its movement—get ever brighter. And then, out of the blue, there's this child again—Dikikh is quite sick of him already, but let him be, thinks Dikikh, stopping politely. The child talks to him, playing with a vine, his hand on his eyes as he tries to shield them from the torturous, sunless light. And if you looked under his hand, you'd see, almost on top of your head, low clouds madly rushing in from the south.

"If you solve a riddle, Dikikh," says the child not in his own voice, "you'll live." And he twists his mouth, as though he had no desire to say such things.

"So you know my name?" says Dikikh in astonishment—more out of cunning than naïveté because he wants to gain some time. "And what if I don't?"

"Come on now! You've been around, lived a long life. You should know better..."

"All right then, let's hear your riddle," Dikikh decides feeling a tickle under his heart.

"Tell us, when will you die?"

"Me?" says Dikikh, "Me?" And he falls silent.

At first he feels inexpressibly sad, but already the next moment says the following:

"Wait... Are you telling me I'll die if I don't tell you when I'll die?"

"Precisely," says the child.

"But what if —let's have it your way—what if I gave you a date and then didn't die when I said I would?"

The child shrugs his shoulders. The dream's expanse starts to shrink with an amazing swiftness. The dream envelops Dikikh powerfully, he finds himself in a dark, light sack, unable to move either a lip, or a hand. Then everything dims, and other dreams enter his dream. There are a lot of them, and they bring a lot (benefit and harm, but most often, nothing), and this "a lot" is of no benefit at all.

I'll never write about this again, because the requirement can't be fulfilled: to what beginning do we attribute ourselves? You slowly and patiently—almost half-heartedly—taught me how to divest us of the straitjacket of "we". It's easier to get accustomed to riches. It's harder to get out of the habit of poverty. For the last time. For the first—or for the hundredth—time carefully reading what was written and changed by unsteadily following the ever vaguer representation of your own desire, you undertake to guess the weak outlines of the appearing object. Only in the weakness of vision—or more precisely, in an ascent to its weakening—is inexhaustible greatness revealed. He was forced to resort to silence. But what was the need? We speak only because we continually desire to understand what we are saying. The ornament of mica ruptures. It happened more often at night, when everyone had departed into (beyond) another time, into (beyond) the time of scalped dreams. It would be much too easy to say that one autumn night when I was 11, I had a dream in which I chanced to sleep with my mother. We submerged our hands in the entrails of a bird. The disposition of organs was favorable. Prepositions determine the trajectories of verbs. Squirming, naked, skinless, dressed in blood, slime, salt, and vomit, with my knees pressed to my chin, I was adrift, between disgust and fear, in a gently whirling stream. A picture from an atlas of human anatomy. I taught the Sirens how to sing, I taught them to hear the basics of digital recording which was to preserve forever the secret ornaments of the journey slashing my body with its pendulum, filling it with an invulnerability settled in a clot of expectation under my heart. Then I stopped writing poetry. There was too little wax left in my soul. Poetry... the kind of poetry that... it had too little violence.

I preferred to write the way dead people read books—backwards, as though they had two-way mirrors in their mouths—or the way time sometimes manifests itself to vision, turning inside out, becoming the sphere of a recklessly self-contemplating eye. Such was their conclusion. Icy basalt surfaces are covered with the cinnabar outlines of a long-forgotten hunt, of blood streaks frozen in caramel radiance. The word "feminine" has too much detail. There are bones here too. Melted honey. Insects reigned in gardens like double-horned moons; the height of their ascent was measured in amber splashes of infinite Chinese scales that covered the square radiating in all ten directions, like an incantation spilling crumbs of dry snow. And the icy arch of those spectacles? And the muffled striking of the clock setting the coordinates for colors, smells, and anticipations? And our whisper, our words losing their meanings a few hours or days later? And the piano etudes of Czerny? And the dahlias, the dew on the wood of the well winch, the distant splash down below, shaped into a glimmering ring that locked our heads together (but without a sound, without a single whiff of wind)— the helplessness of birds and other messengers? And, finally, this: "The less experienced we were in such pleasures, the more ardently we indulged in them, the less they tired us"? How magically one thing followed on from another, continued another, preceding itself in the conscious anticipation of a continuation in the eternal, hovering givenness of the present-tense verb! The video camera was in your room. I'd left the monitor at my place and, lying on the floor, watched you undress (there was water dripping from the ceiling; I also watched wires on the floor) as you glanced at the camera, aware I must be staring at you, aware of my staring at you, of my watching you take off your dress and the rest, and then, instead of lying down, keep standing, feeling increasingly awkward—you were to perform an ordinary thing (the action bracketed as an expression): simply to have an orgasm in front of the camera, as though just for yourself, remaining completely free from any anticipation, yet at the same time being aware that you were "on my side too", viewing yourself with my eyes, moving further and further away from the illusory self-identification—and this is exactly where one sensed the growing tension: between the framing, i.e., myself, and the void replacing your corporeality and pure intention. Does "justice" have anything to do with our experiments? Doubtlessly, to study a law is to change it. The change, the exchange happened inside, like a flame within a flame. You turn your thigh to the camera for a moment—what's behind this movement? Embarrassment, I suppose. Your fear that I might see, on your other thigh, a tattoo the tiniest letters of which form a story about calendars and wanderings among screeching rocks, alive in the mouth, monotonously speaking of the future, one's own future—and what do I care about it, with what thread am I to sew myself to myself? Was there a feeling that the entire idea was useless or pointless? We wanted love. This sentence has no meaning outside a sentence. We wanted a multitude of words. Love was to become the quarrying of ourselves, emerging from a completely different side of the narrative. We deserved to see it face to face, to see it emerging from its own absence—to capture the moment when its preconditions change their own nature, when they promise to become something else, when deafening silence undertakes to fold space. But where were we in those moments? Why didn't we remember anything? Representing ourselves to ourselves was an unmanageable task from the beginning. To continue being a reality while simultaneously becoming its sign that dissembles nothing, only relentlessly elevates itself in a continuous shadow—even in one's sleep, where nothing meant anything, except what one wanted to see in it. I saw, you saw, she saw, we all saw. Where shall we find what was seen? To see means to think; to think means to sleep. Sleep is nothing but a necessary combination of signs. The water's roar grew at the steps; there were yellow manes of foam, wet locks of water in the wind's sharp crest, and the slow, shimmering dissipation of the noise. On the banks—squint, every time!—there are sunny fields of daisies. And our learning to kiss each other in every place, beginning with the toes? Let's keep turning the pages: when you touched your breast with a razor—no, everything could of course be described—"your pupils contracted (this is how one describes it), your breathing stopped for a second, and with a gentle force, slowly, very slowly, you drew a tiny line on your breast. It immediately began to blur with blood (the morning wave of myopia); you bent your head, and when you looked up, I saw your eyes shining with exultation." GREEN VEINS IN TURQUOISE, OR, THE GRAY STEPS LEAD UP UNDER THE CEDARS. Obviously, one should hold on to the musical instrument even in fire.

The sentence described a curve. "I thought," you said with some animation, "I was just about to understand something when it immediately slipped away, leaving my memory with a trace of delightful anticipation." The excessively detailed affirmation of the "feminine" is extremely important—no less so than the skill of oral calculation. But what does it mean then? I don't know. Never thought about it. Much as it is my right, my wish, my desire, my continuous effort "not to distort" the world, this is what always happens. No matter what I say. As usual, I came here again when there was nothing else left for me to do. The old man on a bicycle was swept along into further rain, the fax from a friend was quickly losing coherence—I was free. The university barometer indicated a dry spell. At the department, thanatologists in shorts were drinking beer. There was enough of it to last a while. A grammarian sitting next to them was exhausted with the heat and his own grimace curling the corners of his mouth. Behind the grimace, the mystery of grimy mushrooms slowly unfolded. The grammarian, against all odds, separated the world into what was now accessible (the amount of which he thought was increasing) and the still highly inaccessible. The thanatologists were the keepers of the highly inaccessible. They kept it in the depths of their beer the taste of which stubbornly tried to slip out of the grammarian's mouth. His mouth reminded him of a pumice rabbit-hole that housed aluminum production on a continental scale.

Cherries were in bloom. The corridors were naïve, yellow, and long. They consisted of syncopal transitions between points on a clock dial. The thanatologists treated classicists with reasonable serenity while gently reproaching young Derridians who smoked an incredible deal on the stairs, talking about Fassbinder and the latest scandal. Fassbinder was dead. The scandal was that Lyotard, during a recent visit to Odessa, had apparently started his lecture with an analysis of Berdiaev's late works. Some tended to think it was a simple mistake, and he lectured on Baudrillard. "Both are significant in equal degree," was the hefty verdict of the mightily bearded thanatologist who magically produced a dried bream to accompany the beer and handed it to the grammarian. Some held the opinion that Egypt was the last station. An error is always conscious. Sometimes an error is the result of complex, multi-level operations and calculations. I was given enough beer and time to gather the strength to enter the classroom, sand, and water. Four people were leafing through their notebooks. The rest was as before—corridors, smoke, time, cherries, and memory. The window at the end of the classroom announced military action. A kite fluttered in the deep blue sky. The cry of the fish stuck in my ears like a bone. My work at this university was coming to an end. They once told me it had begun. I approached this end with my typical indifference, but only from the other end. In the end, the work and I missed each other again. My dream vacation was beginning. But you know, dear reader, my heart still quivers every time I remember the place where I could always find shelter. How blissful it was to go to sleep under a blanket that anthropologists readily shared, and listen, while falling asleep, to a distant, sonorous murmur of brandy! Many tried in vain to find the pipe through which it ran day and night. In my time they spoke of the pipe as a vague prophecy awaiting its hour. Some dissertations were almost prepared to make it an archetype of the steam engine, and later, of energy as such. At night, hundreds of thirsty people secretly drilled holes in the walls. Some went insane. The only person who discovered the pipe while repairing the central heating, was Grigory-Tsar-of-Cats, from the office of the Chief Mechanic. But, according to apocryphal evidence, after his serendipitous discovery, Grigory left cats and mechanics to become a monk. A sharply drawn detail was always valued in those parts. It was as though the most important thing was about to slip away, and one needed a precise strategy for putting details on the map—so as accidentally not to get lost in white stones, in the forking of "until next time" and "never"—not that anyone wanted to read something else, to retrace the path, affirming the vanishing by repetition. A reflection is instantaneous, like a simile. A simile is untraceable, because its "second part" doesn't exist. Only the sickle of a pendulum incessantly drew silver trajectories, by weightlessly twisting straight lines and thus continuing a letter once written to a prison. Insects are a line from the book of the dead who endlessly live in dying. But this kind of evidence is extremely scarce. There was little difference between the cities. Now nothing prevents us from talking about it openly. The secret filled us with significance; its presence contained a host of inseparable meanings—an Eden of meanings. I'll never be able (have time) to write about how the pattern of fire is formed in grass faded from a morning frost. In the dusk one could easily guess the outline of the angel of neurosis, or a description that signifies its emptiness, within which no directions are hidden, except the one pointing to the endless anticipation of its own appearance. They said, "the Angel of History..." Understanding is epiphenomenal. Some think this experiment is endless. I'm of a different opinion. I used to try to awaken my compassion for those who inhabited the cities. They pressed hands to their faces, as if trying to hide behind them, but I could clearly see their watchful eyes. Snow wouldn't melt on the gravel road. Remember, it took me some time to learn how to undress you... Three dots signify forgetting, not confusion, as do unforeseen circumstances hindering continuation. It isn't true that the hands know what to do. The snowstorm lasted four days and four nights. But I want to remember whether I *saw* at the moments of, say, aimless (absolute!) "wandering around your body" what my hands were finding. And did this connect to the images that, until then, possessed my imagination so effortlessly? In what way were you combined with the one who existed before—but of course, also thanks to—you? The tarnished tansy, the celestial turning of bicycle wheels, the solar investigation. Murder, like a timber-worm, worked its way through the mass of bewilderment.

It determined the borders of durations and bad weather. But I had no news of any kind for them. Silent gongs answered the air by the wall of a disproportionately tall building. Their sound was falsely geometrical. We listened to Tibetan exiles on Californian hills at dawn. They earnestly claimed they were continuing a philosophical debate started in 1439 at the newly built Datsan of Zhud Mad, with Sherab Senge attending in person. Some say the abundance of sweat exerted in a debate doesn't bring one closer to enlightenment. But the world consists of false signs of presence, and only the prick of a straw to the top of your head allows you to see what knowledge and prayer are powerless to deliver. Purple, wide sleeves, chins, burning gasoline. Charcoal-black birds with crimson tussocks hovered in the radiant spheres of vibration by the top ledges of the building. The air, scorched by insatiable transparency, brought things closer to their origin in the pupils of our eyes. We couldn't see very much from below, but I noticed a few people. One of them, seated in a chair, was wearing a dark suit inappropriate for such a hot evening. Holding on to the back of his chair, there stood another, with an open book in his hand. His facial type gave food for thought. There was a third one too. I saw sapphire reflections from a distant flame glinting on their faces, on the carpets covering the roof, and on the pages of the open book, flying around with the crackling of torn silk. Ships may have been burning in the port. For a moment, I had envisioned a strange city I hadn't seen before. And strangely, it seemed I had always known that this city was in the north, that its nights were a mirror reflection of its days, that I myself wasn't really walking among the gray, deserted houses, but, as it were, sailing in a light vessel of an unfamiliar type, with its sails consumed by these ghostly flames. I even thought I could hear snippets of a conversation. Someone's voice pronounced, "everything happens as if it were sleepy guesswork…, a place that can describe neither result, nor prerequisites." Listening to the words that vaguely reminded me of something, all of a sudden I saw myself stretch out my hand to the fire involuntarily. The flame didn't burn. This sensation must have frightened away the delusion. It didn't seem to have lasted very long. Pungent, hot dust smoking underfoot finally brought me to my senses. I looked around—glass cages with children inside followed the main column on wooden wheels in strict files. Banners fluttered rhythmically in the incandescent, milky haze.

We were escorting the planets to another exile. And there was something else: a waving of hands. As if we were being greeted, though it was obvious we were leaving the city. It may have appeared we were departing, crossing the imaginary line of a fantasized defeat which immortality always turned into, even in dreams. I heard a soft voice saying, "One had to live a life to understand everything not as others understood it..." And another voice replying, "But is what I'm saying something my speech 'transported' from the region of intention to the prismatic spectrum of language, to the body of its meanings where any of my meanings are drawn, unfolding their relations?" A lie is just a correction for parallax. Strings taut in the mouth shimmered with the tremor of split consequences and the dark rainbows of mercury not transubstantiated into double mirrors. Like ridiculously hasty statements. Like brown on pink. Like rain on the face. Like the known in the unknown. Like a nightingale. Like the "where" of "always". Mountains got closer, but nothing changed the proportions in the interrelations of sound and memory. The porcelain purity of the outskirts in the chipped distance between things escalated the frequency of transmitting vibrations. There weren't enough of them for thought to rest, as on the support of a further movement along nameless slopes, but quite enough to mutely decorate any outside movement with delightful operatic cordage. A tiny thing separates man from himself: language. Tirelessly he begs the skies to relieve him from it. The skies additionally serve as an inconspicuous difference as they don't allow man to disappear in his appeal to them. Even when he doesn't specify who is making the appeal and why. Sometimes you dream you're pulling a splinter. It's enormous, endless—you roll yourself up and are left with nothing but dizziness and a weak attempt to grab the edge of the bed. Not the best consolation. Sometimes a question coincides with an answer.

Their customs initially caused understandable disappointment, but after a while, their inescapable uselessness began to fascinate more and more, hindering one's conduct. I remembered city streets, endless Slavic expanses of windowsills and corridors. Besides, I suspected that we were dealt the same cards day after day. Wide rivers of sand embraced the city from the north, where plateaus, uprooted by a tornado, were slowly burning. The art of panhandling was under the state's official patronage. It was the nation's all—its literature, history, and in part, philosophy and theology. Yet, if they were familiar with Plato, they'd certainly declare themselves followers of the Socratic tradition. Local trees had no leaves but bloomed once in eleven years. Such was the cycle of a petition's becoming a reciprocal gift. A week had eleven days; the same eleven months lay between conception and birth; human life was marked by the simple number 11—mirrored in the figure of its own inscription, resembling two arrows meeting in a flight of unknown origin. In eleven, I thought, they retained the monad of one, without abasing it by condescending to division. It all depends on how you write it down.

They liked theater, gossip, dull wine born of fruit tasting like acacia flowers (those of a certain particular fig tree unknown in the north); they were indifferent to deceptions and problems of immortality. They relieved themselves lying down. Running was forbidden. God was allowed to exist as a false memory. One of the artists, shaven-headed and faceless like a morning shadow, once helped me to publish a book of my observations: the thinnest sheet of steel the size of a sail was cut through with a few letters; wind was whirling in them (CLOSE READING), while another wind—from the mountains—played with the gigantic steel sheet itself. Two readings. I thanked him, vaguely remembering the humming silver books of my childhood and the apples on which we used to tell our fortunes. Surprisingly, they were familiar with the boomerang. At first I thought it was the manifestation of the eternal rotation of the letter, or rather a hieroglyph, but then abandoned the thought as redundant. It was the boomerang—eleven of them, to be precise—revolving under the dome of the structure where transgressors were judged, that made up the image of the universe. Now you understand why I mistook the boomerang for a letter at first. Violators of public morals periodically lay claim to origin—they called for the casting down of old idols, the introduction of new rules of chronology, and the giving away of one's property to others without being asked for it. Gods walked the streets in alabaster masks; their bones were surprisingly weak and pliable. Any woman could stop a god and strangle him if she wished. This, in turn, caused the indignation and fierce opposition of the people who couldn't imagine how the beauty they possessed undividedly throughout their history—according to principles of petition which stipulated that the supplicant shall receive the gift of beauty—could be sacrificed to someone's overgrown pride. Collections of embalmed gods overflowed museums. But the indignation never stepped outside the limits of pure theorizing. It's naïve to think that the concept of petition, entreaty, upon which these people's ethics and worldview were founded, was similar to the philosophy of privation. "The boomerang acquires its destructive power only by its correct return trajectory"—this dictum was rather popular while we were there. One was supposed to sing it, clapping one's hands. Sometimes, without any effort, and very unexpectedly for others, they went on to make even more absurd, simply ludicrous statements. They would start talking with barely comprehensible fear about some endless matrix in which another one—the matrix of the limit, i.e., "the end of the world" embodied by all the dead—is concealed. The tonal system of the language allowed them to sing anything at all. Including the notion that the convergence of these two limits yields a third one: absolutely unlimited space.

We were invited to learn two things. The first was to sleep at night (we had to create night). The second... I remember nothing about the second. I walked out of the office and waved to the guard; it rained. One could stroll down Liteiny to the neighborhood where my house was—or rather, the remains of my studio apartment, a 20-minute walk away. The apartment consisted of a window, a kitchen table in the kitchen, and a computer assembled by Fr. Lob who was always on line. Sometimes it also consisted of Karl and Fr. Lob. V uglu byla postel'. From the window, as I dreamed sometimes, one could see the same apartment with snow falling behind its window. Let's not talk about it.

It's incredible how small the range of characters is, how much books diminish in size.

I should have visited Karl first, but I realized I'd forgotten again what he was doing. Water was pouring down my collar. The cold air was pleasant. Unconcerned, I smoked, standing on the bridge above the district stretching out below where lights already twinkled in the fog. This place was still called "the Neva". Some still remember the photographs from the time when swelling water heavily glistened here, instead of residential blocks and the rest. Nothing was left from that age. Except bridges. And who doesn't pity it? No one knows what's closer to one's heart, water or electricity, or for example, electricity or death.

The eyelid sinks; a unicorn marches through the blizzard of the blade.

Of course, you learn the taste of wine over again, under the banners of the same old wind. The night's bowl boiling in hoarfrost—what are the eyes that close eyelashes incinerated by snow? My hand (hearing, vaguely); the weight of the fir tree branches under the snow. Frost boiling in birds' dry burns—what eyes remain here, in the fissures of things, in the pores of their substance and shadows, still burdened with their weightless load? Whirlwinds intricately move in from mushroom-rich suburbs, frizzling red sand in cocoons of flashes, allowing desire to see itself in the folds of sleeplessness as pure tension that can open "one thing" to "another", imprisoning the indistinct movement of lips (and another return to airy, brass speech) in the lentil ice of vigilance, acids, approach, invisibility. Petunias, granite, weak bindweed on a whitewashed wall, angels carved in sugar, track-laying threads of mirror conjunctions above the dark river of fire carrying dry twigs, uprooted grass, corpses of resemblance, and bodies whose faces are read by the green half-moon that relieves the reading with its grin, as though fingers would never again shape the same hands, palms, and eyes, dropping them like apples into a bottomless fall blooming on the edge of shamrock and touch, on the limit of sedge clay and breath that collects one or several syllables in the sharp point of an imaginary target, painfully oblivious to them in its cleansing mutter, akin to the dark rivers of fire and the salty, warm fog from shallow waters. A thousand-armed sun tears down the sails of one thing returning to the next—sails of what's understood as change. But here you are transparent and similar to wine. One step from this—one page from the sentence just inscribed—

lies what can manifest itself in any metaphor—is this not what the writer aims for, is it not the circuitous, oblique escape path to the origin, to the all-forgiving beginning? For only in its perspective is he likely to feel the incomparable taste of futility and fruitlessness of the origin with which he merges—to feel the unfeasibility of any birth. Is this not what the writer seeks? Doesn't he seek that which in one way or another appropriates names of death—granted that its names, gender endings, and other accessories have no number, or rather do, but on the near side, as it were, at the point of beginning, becoming, shifting, even as they expend everything—including names— to the very last drop in their approach to names, numbers, and intention? In the same way, the project of "love" is infused with the energy of loss as the inspiring secret of experience that doesn't lock on to any single choice, notion, or knowledge defined as something not realizable, not real, not subject to reality—as though knowledge could deliberately run ahead of its own anticipation. It is then that we say "love" or something else if it drizzles, or if dry leaves and sleeping birds are blown in from the harbor through the crowns of strung trees, wounded by monotony.

I often happened to encounter many/much. Including this beautiful staircase, showing up white, like a chunk of the Crimea underneath a veil of impenetrable blue. Bridges ceased to be the linking elements of the landscape; they'd been separated from what they connected. Streetwalkers like me. We departed. Did we! Then we arrived. Some returned, despite adversative conjunctions. Reproaches addressed to them are groundless. Others contented themselves with modest exercises resulting in huge but incredibly fragile machinery. Our bodies are dissimilar. I agree, except perhaps that our skin may be found similar... yes, almost identical, apart from a turtle tattoo on my left shoulder and an endless narrative on your thigh, whose letters swiftly shrink their outline, erasing any possible interpretation from the surface of imagination, becoming atoms of your blood, pores of sense that circulates unhindered in the exchange of such substances as saliva, dreams, and memory, altering the combinations of their components, shaping your bodily frame, skeleton—*skia*—something antecedent, like times revealed at a given moment—such are ecstasy, exchange, change, the sweetest, motionless leap—a narrative that precedes you and everything, while you are just a rind signifying what awaited you from early childhood, or an even less comprehensible time. It's an ordinary evening. Orderly in its distribution of light. On whose left shoulder? Movement is the last illusion left over from the pharmacological age. I wonder what's inside this skin. Bones. An abundance of moisture, liquid. Some think it's under the skin that the soul is found, hiding in the forest of bones and molecules. The blueprints of their disposition are kept in the foothills of upstate New York. Interestingly, no one was consumed by envy. The moon's mercury sphere guarded the eye's pupil and waned in its retreat behind the eyeball. The mouth observed the aging of speech, its gaps. I never did. Vision has its own hidden motive. Is the object of your vision separate from you or is it inscribed in your "readerly narcissism" as an excrescence of the collective project? Where are they? At least, how many are they? Are they beautiful, smart? Are they recognizable? My writing is a prime example of late-twentieth-century classicism. However, it's simply impossible to see anything even at a closer look. It's just that we weren't here then. To move through the muslin of sleep. Feeling with the hands. Taking possession without a touch. The machinery of sense generation is the description of abstract repetitions, of their territories.

Is repetition possible without that which repeats in it? And finally: the fall of the knife illuminated the motionless bird with the burning magnesium of vertigo. The fall of the bird divided vision in two: brass and letter. People on the roof started moving but didn't look up; we walked, leaving this cursed place as we'd left other, similar places, and the smell of fresh cinders relentlessly followed us. This is why the letters had to be carved through, they had to be a particular substance: void. Nothing can become a trace. But we'd learned to give them the shape of nothing, coordinating matter with our whims.

Such, too, are my memories, gathered with a "special purpose". In one of the purposes, everything is indivisible, in the other, everything is as though in front of itself, unmarked, unrecognized, even if felt by hands without touching. We were called upon as the rulers of knowledge, but the term of the contract expired. The juice of spurge drips from a cut stem. The end of the lunar lactation period coincided with the beginning of a solar eclipse. For this reason many of the people up high shrank back from the edge. Which could obviously mean the loss of composure. At the very beginning we agreed to develop the theme of urban loneliness and got on with it like the widow of a man with the best theater seat. We were least of all interested in the psychoanalytical aspects of comparison. They suggested a change of terminology. Grammatical categories of number. We continued our measured movement. Beggars were tumbling down into the moisture of a head wind, resembling shivering tinfoil figures from a shooting gallery, beaded on the slippery thread of a gunshot. How much did you put in an outstretched hand today? Tulips were in bloom; Tibetan prayer wheels rolled their cylinders, abuzz with bees beguiled by the future.

My love slipped out of you, leaving neither a trace, nor a yesterday, nor a now. We realized that we needed ourselves for comparison—as its second part. Immediately I thought you were glass with which my mouth has fused. I touched you, overcoming disgust; otherwise we couldn't have achieved the purpose of our meeting. The ray of your fall carved out a hovering knife that reflected the bird and the fish in burning magnesium.

Wounds exhaled the fragrance of gillyflower, hot wax, and vomit. "Does it really hurt?" you asked. We will leave these parts and become shells with threatening edges, a vague noise locked in the very middle, in the void that conceives our interminable transformation.

Bruises, fingertips rubbed to bleeding, crumbling shell rock, wheels running downhill. Tails of hot Provence dust. Red sage, immortelle, and mint. That's enough, you said, and went to the shower. An electric fan celebrated by Homer. We crawled across the floor, picking up fluttering pages. India ink is skillful in its stupor, but that's how color shrinks to recognition in a spasm—like ivy on a blind courtyard wall. But we've only just approached what happened at the time when we both learned to undress each other, or in other words, not to pay heed to the process. History burned away with the sluggishness of ink on the straw-colored underwings of insects. We talked about apathy and disgust.

"The insane also grow old," I said. I was in no hurry.

To which you replied:

"The absence of logic may be effortlessly contained in a certain logic of elimination."

"And what was the logic of our behavior on the farm? " It was an old, nearly forgotten story of the beginning of our love, when once at night, without a word, we grappled naked in the cowshed mud—I remember the taste of the manure we rolled in, how she screamed that this was exactly what it took to understand why we still needed each other, if at all—then her hands became weaker, and only our breath was heard.

"There can never be too much death," she said a day later while cutting my hair, "and by the way, I didn't notice," she continued, "whether you came or not... Not that it really mattered." I just shrugged my shoulders beneath the sheet she covered me with. "And not that we *had* to do it at all, but it is, of course, a matter of principle," she added, and then, in a few minutes, "say something at least! Why the hell are you silent? Say it feels good when I cut your hair, or something." A few years later I told her we hadn't had to go anywhere and that our old fun seemed as innocent as paper roses now. Roses are roses, she replied, and her vacant look made it clear her thoughts were elsewhere.

Breathing is getting stronger. A cloud. And city-dwellers who know very well that only a word separates them from each other and from themselves. A ghostly obstacle of ghostly times. Are they happy? But you, why are you also lost in these rows and crowds, silently standing on both sides of the staircase that leads to the shore? Yes, in this case inarticulateness is quite forgivable. Obviously, at night I caught myself again understanding nothing in a book open before my eyes. An explanation unfolding the next explanation—such is the informational strategy of society. Methods of explanation differ, but they're common in the explicit intention to open the mechanisms of meaning production (at best, those of law). But because it happens in a constant displacement, explanation is an act the result of which from the outset needs explaining as a new given. This is the context where we find the known illusion of integrating information (for obvious reasons "understanding" is not to be used here as a term)—in other words, a comprehensive picture of what is happening. Even without rising up to a stricter level of "proof", the principle of explanation is the governing one. It bores me to talk about it further.

The book ingratiatingly turned my pages, page after page—all of them were empty and yet thickly filled with lines. The chirping past illuminated dust dappled with the fast-hand of Nashq desert. Midbar. The history of these parts goes back to the age of oceanic retreat, of shell-formation, and the formation of blood on a potter's wheel. Hand me a sweater, a knife, salt, a cup, bread, blood—anything. That's what I want. Heavens, what a warm evening! How long ago it all was. How enchanting was the quiet wind swaying field flowers in the dusk. Chance and choice govern nothing; even if someone's memoirs say they do, it only means one thing: only under specific conditions, where alternatives are obedient to the government of opposition. Forgive the awkwardness. It can't be that I used to embrace you differently. How? What was around us? What occupied our heads? Ourselves? And our hands? Have they changed? Someone is knocking. Great, someone has brought us money and wine. If in the early '60s we'd known mushrooms, we'd never have experienced the taste of true melancholia, enchanting dust, and the last rays of the day, burning away on the rocks. Is it worth descending to hell only to begin missing it in the end? It's a question of time. An answer of space. Any enumeration expends itself in its growth and thus acquires the critical mass of reliability. I don't think so. Concentrate on your toes. Everything shines. Blinding luster, intolerable to hearing! It requires blind faith. Such is night. Such is plague. The same incandescent, but already immaterial leaves drift in from the Milky Way. Trees shed whirlwinds of leaves. I don't understand what's more important: to know "how" or "why". Even in a close, lateral scrutiny of the crystalline noise formations. The saturation of the narrative happens in reverse. From here we move to the third line, and the expectation inscribes a few words that are unnecessary or have little meaning. Prices went up. But not so much as to put one at a loss or to make one lose one's head. I remember how I vowed (dissonance) never to let you out of my arms. And what did we lose in the end? A few cheap stories? Then words slowly join edges (the production of purest forms, beyond all greed) and make up a sentence that has no completion in intention. At the same time, what comes first—the intention of the word or the word exacting intention? Such a sentence is ready to dissolve, to lose certain "property" in any environment. As I, for example, or you. Here are your documents, bitch. No, Vera Sergeyevna, I don't like your plan. Of course, I can surf their networks, but that won't help us. She wasn't... ok, she *is* one of those who prefer to keep their money in the bank. How shall we do it? As if you didn't know, poor thing! Fine, let's say it'll be my little secret. Incidentally, where are you going this evening? No, I don't insist. Why should I? You're the boss, you pay me. By the way, someone called you today a few times. He wouldn't give his name. No, fuck it, every time I asked, they hung up. Of course I'm sure, no one is interested in my person. (No, having a go at the bank networks was no problem; I just needed to get in touch with those Dortmund cowboys, and loop back to myself through them. Too bad, damn it, too bad Karl had gone off on his stupid journey to the "dead").

Or the duration of money. I know (or I'd like to think) I habitually don't hear words: consequently, this is how you turn towards me, light from the window (who is it for?) falls on your face, you slowly (more slowly) raise your hand, as though you wanted to stop yourself, and I'm not going to interrupt you—I have nothing to say—that is, I seem to have said what was required: "why children cry"; I would have given a lot to be able to say (first, to want to say...) something else to you, and then... no, again I can't hear a thing. Whom are you talking to all this time? Whom are you addressing? Doctors? It's better to see. Get off the phone! I smoke a lot. At my age one should be doing something else. Nobody owns anything in all houses without exception. I arrive (now the searching mind can place signs on the dim cobweb—arrival, parting... incidentally, not particularly reliable markers). How disgusting the smell of these suffocated, rotting roses. I don't want to think of anyone. Everything written is written not to return to what's written. The strangulation furrow of northern distinction. The slow bifurcation into "I" and "you" is usually a sign of weakness. There are always those who are never there and have never been. How is this object different from another one—from "Galileo", for example? The question may be put differently: what in this object allows "me" to think it, expend it into my presence, and, if this is really so (the introduced word *reality* is "obviously" the shadow of the virtual reality of unattached words whose referential spirals never locked in the point of a definite meaning; the train doesn't stop at this station; one can look out of the window at the inscriptions laid out on the embankment, but we're interested in intonation—that's what ought to be chosen between the sphere of recognizability and the dissolution in the non-obvious), if this isn't the result of an external insistence, then what changes does this fact undergo in my experience as I continue to answer the object's own invitation to think (imagine, experience, perceive, etc.) it? The most sincere answer is supposedly this: I don't know what a *named* object is. Of course, I don't know this until it's named. But the following answer is also legitimate: I don't know what *this* named object is either. At some point its name, its presence in my experience, i.e., my knowledge of it stops to satisfy me; furthermore, it becomes absolutely inadequate to itself at the moment of asking. The question always destroys the answer. Well, of course, one could remind oneself much about many things or, at least make up some scenes from early childhood.

Actions, order. It's not difficult to see collected works of any color on the shelves, a stuffed bird, formulae crackling like kites when touched by hot air. Moist turf underfoot. In our case, to speak of corporeality/body doesn't mean to speak of it as property/substance, i.e. as the sphere of becoming in the usual sense. Sparkle. Can't touch. Like the squeaking door—the curvature and increase of tension. The smell of paper and printer's ink is amazing. Gravel, interval, the flow of microelements in the cellular substitution of sacred texts—the shifting of forms. Also lines, isolated stanzas, chapters. You can. But you shouldn't get involved in the action that describes a ban on involvement. Islands. Birds. I catch myself wondering (permission, submission to reading) who possesses the words that describe the destruction of the answer in the question? I who hold the book in my hand, as I walk down a chalk staircase to the water? Paper that holds scattered signs, thanks to some chemical laws of cohesion and interaction? Magic that transforms rows of type into something the imagination produces during such transformation?... What makes a thing a thing? The purity of the sign is determined by the imaginary reflectivity of the plane on both sides of the grimace "equation". Is death determined by the origin of its arrival? The production of pure money depends on the atmospheric conditions. I prefer to think of the physical reality of the body as some intentional "clot" (although at some point I become aware that my body takes place in the process of "neutralization"—i.e. outside a relation to whether it exists in reality!)—who I am, thinking my body—or as an endless possibility of anticipating any thing (including myself) that my consciousness produces in the course of perceiving/desiring this very thing. But what appears in the imagination? Same thing in mine as in another's? The complete absurdity of action in approximation: a deviation into history, signs of an "alternation" of nations, incisions, erasing what's called action in the absence of action—thing, or speech addressed to speech. A descent into Hades is the metaphor for constructing a computer sign, which in turn assumes the following: is common knowledge probable? Do you feel the same thing as I do during our embraces or talks? How to compare parts of our experience? *What* leaves us *what*? Or: do both parts constitute a oneness that exists independently from number? OK, let's assume that corporeality is the horizon of my (my body's) expectation of the attendant world—the floating (re)partition of the surrounding world, extracting this world from the absence in experience of endless discernment. But what is the *similar* that again and again forces us to experience it, as though *common* knowledge were our property—that which would allow me to talk of this object with an Other (this Other is finally circumscribed), sharing it in the process of comprehending knowledge and each other in knowledge? Then it's much easier for me to view corporeality/body as a certain border that has neither interior, nor exterior—that is, as a certain permanent syntactic operation of producing myself and the Other.

Still, how disgusting is the smell of suffocated roses.

It is not obliqueness but vision stiffening on the insurmountable approaches to a thing, no matter in what "is" this thing hides its limits.

In an hour, Dikikh was lying on a mattress.

A TV was in front of him on the floor. Floating across the screen was a cloud floating behind the window, along the stearin plane of the glass stiffening within the limits of the permitted shift in presentations. A phone rang on the floor by the door. Dikikh didn't turn to the ring. Neither did I. I was thinking about the university and the universe. Fr. Lob closely followed the photograph and the action unfolding in it. He moved his finger, lips, and sometimes exclaimed words that weren't particularly coherent to others. Karl was further on his way into the desert which fitted into the unthinkably subtle touch of a needle or number (the ideal desert is always behind you), and his body, stretched out on a sweaty sheet (no one changed it for him for two months in a row), was occasionally convulsed by a weightless spasm.

"Clouds float above him," said Fr. Lob.

"Something in him is still attached to something," he said in a while.

We talked about poetry because it had nothing attached to anything already; it appeared as a pure sphere of rarefied abstractness. Its borders pulsated, but nothing shaped behind them. Clouds descended on the slopes. Talking about poetry was an activity full of profound significance because its meaning was in no way transformed into the action of its pulsating borders.

White clouds were rushing across the blinding blue sky with a terrifying power. We observed the picture, spellbound. It was getting larger. Its seed grew; the pores of its destruction, joyful like recognition, were penetrated by the spores of other representations, beginning to disseminate possible images—yet what was to follow them certainly lagged. In a washed-clean space, Kirpichny Lane seemed desolate from the heat. The sharp, intolerable light flooded every dent on the walls and every crack in the asphalt. White grass grew in the walls and pavement. We saw Dikikh see himself walking down the lane. Then he became the walking person. This was of no benefit at all.

He walked up to the window where the child—no, the freak, the old man... no, rather, the child—once sat. The window was shut. In the mirror-like glass the same clouds floated swiftly through the darkened, hot sky. Dikikh leaned up against the windowpane and slowly started to make out the inside of the room through the suddenly animate blue streaks.

The room was filled with boxes; there was a camcorder hoisted on a tripod by the second window. Someone was lying on a mattress by the wall.

A TV was in front of the person. On the screen, clouds were falling down swiftly, and behind them the sky turned into a ravishing, dark abyss.

A voice said, "You'll never know how the quick brown fox jumps over the lazy dog."

"It's Karl," Fr. Lob surmised.

I didn't answer. The making of every poetic construction became for me the creation of precision mechanics through which one perceives a certain phenomenon we call poetry residing in the sphere of the real. It's organs unfolding outwards.

The voice continued to reason,

"Nowadays, when time hides in homes, like sand after a hurricane, when time is exhausted from sleep, I too want to answer the question about the state of window frames, of city transport, and the migration of seaweed. I'm also putting forward the question about the change of bird routes, but I don't know where the answers are mine and where they're someone else's. Besides, it's important to understand how money differs from, say, words, or meat."

A phone rang in the room behind the window. Before our very eyes, the person on the mattress reached out to get it.

"Don't pick it up," said Dikikh and woke at the

sound of his own voice.

We were silent. Sweat ran down his face. You know what a hot summer in Petersburg is like. Static flickered on the TV screen. The tape had ended.

Dikikh got up from the mattress, walked over to the kitchen cupboard and opened the doors. The cupboard was tightly stuffed with bundles of money. Dikikh opened the box. There was money in it too. Sameness.

"In the end, pleasure excludes the possibility of joy," said Dikikh and grinned at the echo that dashed through the apartment.

"This is my apartment," I said. "I don't like other people in it without permission."

Fr. Lob frowned, looking down at Sennaya Square, but couldn't think of anything to say. In a slow doubling of our images in time, I recognized the somewhat unclear but definitely familiar thought that no action could be viewed as meaningless—even if partially. No matter how strange it is or seems, no matter what monstrously unintelligible reasons cause it (reasons are also among the factors supposedly depriving the action of its obviousness), it's instantly filled with meaning, as wood chips caught in a stream immediately assume its direction and speed—like a word doomed to *restitutio omnium* at the moment of its appearance. It's possible to imagine the moment of the "first" word's emergence—before "all possible further" words—but then it's also quite possible to assume that it contains the meanings of all future words, or the absence of the future as such, for this word is perfect in its imaginary, finite emptiness. The idea of a word that means nothing, is nothing—not even itself—is similar to the idea of universal language; it will never cease to obsess. History knows many efforts, rather insane in their impetuousness, to find and extract this empty word. It isn't possible. Pessimism all the way through. A game of horror and hope. We always come to a destination, much as experience deceptively promises its absence. But absence isn't possible either. Many melancholy tales tell us so, and only children's dreams resist this knowledge for a while. *Angelus Novus.*

He approached the window again. The windows faced the Fontanka. Soon the icy, feather-like stone of the steps will bring back whispers, rustling, and light radiating between water and sky. Further out, there are shrubs, lattices shedding weight, bitterness in the mouth, and dawn like a figure of spoiled speech. Below was his motor boat covered with a dirty tarpaulin. For the rest of the night, Dikikh cut the strings on the boxes. Each was packed with money. He took the money to the kitchen, and then, as if on reflection, back again.

I wasn't there. I couldn't help him avoid the common error.

"Of course not," said Fr. Lob, "you couldn't have done it."

"But why?" I asked, surprised. "Because your thoughts were occupied with Tantalus."

Yet, it didn't happen. A story finds its continuation in another story. A beaten path. It separates from intention. Separation from intention. Do we remember this? Reflection doesn't find its reflection in continuation. It didn't happen. Intransitivity shows up again. Continuation doesn't always require stretching out. A trembling arch of swallows in a smoky September sky (the lemon patina slows down the movement of color elements). Such is offering. The one-dimensional intimacy of the expression "*do you remember?*" crumbles before an aperture, stairwell, ice-hole peeling paint and ashes of a shedding, crumbling body: "*no, I don't remember*". I understand. Further, we have a fiction, as though fashioned from clay, a fossilized honeycomb of fiction, nocturnal stairs to the sea (a considerable time was allotted to the lot of studying cracks in shell rock). We shall build a state of a new kind. As soon as possible. Tomorrow. Ideology is just a dictionary. Dictionary, vision equal desire. Night doesn't enter the equation. Equilibrium is ready to evaporate at any moment. Like peonies, states of a new kind at morning's noon. Countries of proud, happy people full of human dignity—people thinking in the categories of the inhumanly beautiful before an ice-hole, premonition, stair-well in the talus of beginnings, leading to ziggurats of wasps. Then he hears: "each" flame conceals the outline of all burnt things (burnt in the Future Im/perfect). If you turn to the light, I'll be able to tell you how your hair appears to me when you're excluded by movement, when it falls on your face, when a proposed agreement doesn't promise to become fundamental on the condition that you (later) close your eyes, hold your breath, allow me to lean towards you and, when you lie down, press my lips to the spot (opening its continuation in another story) where your heart beats, when the hair of already-knowledge that barely separates us is dissected by our contempt for it and by the silence, growing towards the focus of arrogant removal. Windowpane, grazing roses. Like the skin of vision: neither separating, nor conjoining, where a thing nonetheless ascends in its dimensions and phenomenality, while in fact, the gaze is turned to the outlines of things that flow endlessly into each other in a speculative figure, like a riverbed with multiple streams, only vaguely resembling matter. For the sake of convenience. Isn't it so? One thing is inserted in another. Bodilessness in bodilessness. Nothing else is interesting. Then he hears a response: does "*each*" exist? Is there a flame that differs from another flame? What qualities, say, must "one" flame possess to be distinguishable from "another" flame that *never existed* in the first flame's metaphor of blinding—a metaphor that doesn't produce additional meaning but glides along the trajectory of obliqueness, in order finally to touch the words: "flame", "night"? As well as other words, no less essential for continuing the narrative.

Are we talking about proper names? Names that appropriate and nominate nothing? As nothing is appropriated by the ringing foliation of correctly distributed hopes. The bleeding heart of a peacock. It's better to look at water. This way you understand a lot, even if everything is written out in one line. The distribution of things determines hearing. There are proofs that the whole is divided in multitudes, but these proofs are as obvious as they are unconvincing. The division of a page—a group of words, a word, a letter, a cell of assumed space—by the consuming presentation of intention. The presentation of a murder in three acts, arsons, tenses, and persons. Incidentally, color. Or, quantitative characteristics preceding the equation of burning, to say nothing of chemical processes, underground benzene rings, and the necklaces of Hades shimmering in a sunray that falls, accidentally, on the floor through a crack in the shutters. Garbage bins became a problem for the neighborhood residents. We opened our palms, and the black butterfly of eclipse found temporary refuge in them. In the rustling of sedge, in the hissing of reeds, in the overflowing of sands, forms, and meanings. The floor is dented and flushed. Then he hears: flame is an echo of meanings, rushing towards the origins formed by its own shadow; meanwhile, he thinks: like peonies one morning in July, immobilized by unexpected heat. The *trompe l'oeil* of skies. The Phrygian gates of photography shut, issuing to the eye's pupil the ever-increasing graininess of the real. The city authorities are increasingly concerned about the destroyed system of burials. Cemeteries are entirely social. We penetrate the pores of the indubitable. Sediment. Then, at the strictly designated time, a wind begins to blow, similar to. But what do we remember about it, or about anything else, similar? Gardens of erosion, as if. We'll return to them later, as. To flowers, the amazing and horrifyingly beautiful bodies of calculations, and to bees, as though. If we return at all, akin. Since the wet, dented staircase leads nowhere. Because. That's why.

It wouldn't be hard to climb it up to the attic, which is something else already. I don't like this. But it's all right otherwise …

Then he begins to realize that his ability to set in motion shells of words imbued with the peculiar taste of the desert (but of course, in this motion we'll find room for anything under the sun, including the description of love: an arbitrary July, cloudy, all-absorbing light, elementary particles, amber, and wool), his ability to foresee possible conjunctions, answers the question which of the following words seem more "beloved" than others (this is how the question was once formulated; the graphic examples exacted by [illegible] … I don't understand what could have been written here; no, let's leave it the way it is): amber, glass-like vowels, torn edges, and dust.

You licked blood off my chest. A glass fragment hung existentially (the essential delimitation of the visible and the invisible) in the vibrating razor blade, consuming microspaces of the mediastinum, fires of language. Not of words. There were no words in the region from which echo brought belated, and hence invariably annoying evidence. There were only directions, as if someone—Arakava, for instance—had sent you a letter on a razor edge thirsting for the limit. Only directions, glimpses of the instantly imagined pre-form: we need them to speak about the indestructible equilibrium maintained by their speed. Here I'm restrained by the lack of money and the tenderness for the soiled corner of two streets, the merging point of two suns. We'll discuss their names later. Why do they so persistently wish to have their lives (or at least, the lives of similar people) portrayed in novels, intricate narratives, and films? What do they stand to gain from this? Tell me, tell me, don't hide it all. An intention intentionally lets any fact slip away as an all-too-easy catch. This goes on until the vibrating force fields remain the only fact that must be captured for a subsequent transformation. Here there's no place for motivation. Here there's no place to even put down a glass of beer. He finishes reluctantly, "When once I was asked which words I liked better than others, I said: those that never assumed (or rejected) any meaning in any way related to man." If you think about it, such words are many. One should learn to use them in order to see what follows what. They talked, but what became more ancient than all words, all sentences and utterances—more ancient than writing and the voluptuousness of fingers letting through the dry current of letters and sand, more ancient than vision, since time immemorial implanted in the scull by a spell on water where the echo of what's pronounced multiplies times and where regions of the *nameless* cast no shadows, self-illuminate, and thus prevent language from discerning, untangling, capturing, and delivering that which could have been made later its own property—was the very same words, sentences, their recording, and so on. Don't run so fast, I'm not young anymore. The "color" black. The world of visions and dreams separated these regions from "you", therefore all those who intended to walk it to the end and those who in fact did so, lost any remaining bits of reason on encountering the indifferent, impenetrable fire—or one may say, ice, or a collection of Italian Quattrocento paintings, a collection of shells for a TT handgun—whatever you like, young man, IT'S UP TO YOU. Morning came. This time without its characteristic tardiness.

Yes, finally, I'd like to become a naked function of literal aimlessness. Of letteral typelessness. I even suppose that thanks to this, I'll sooner or later acquire the ability to become invisible or understand something about love. No one's asking you, though. Where, then, does his money come from? But no, the question was about something else. The favorite ones (last year we were talking about words) are those without a single remaining human trace, without a single mark of presence. Traceless ones. Like the melting of fingerprints on a glass, like the whiff of a wind that changes nothing, akin to a shift in the spectrum of meaning, touching flowers, rocks, diminution, tree-bark, disintegration, an amazing flap of a bird's wing that never approached eyelashes, like the weight of a drop and its fall, like the mathematical body of wine. Washed, stiffened linen, flapping in the wind. The borders of a diminutive figure intricately smolder by the line of a nameless space, of its endlessly destroyed equilibrium. The folded line is attached to the thing blindly; the thing eludes contour, outline. The contract of service is discontinued. Contraction is as beautiful as waning hearing. As usual, your lips are a bit salty. To be on the riverbank, in the state of waning, parting, partitioning, diminishing, murmur. It's better this way. It's relatively better to walk through the splashing walls of washed linen—it's the attic for which there is neither desire, nor a word: *what* do you feel there? *what sort* of premonitions does it stir in you, grammatical second person? In the morning, still in the dark, he wrote poems, starting each with "I greet you, Captain Lob!" Once they were neighbors.

And what's there to remember?

Indeed—*what, how* must be remembered, and most importantly, *who* must remember? I'm not writing this because what's written doesn't exist from the beginning. Curiously, however (says someone addressing himself), it is *I who talks* to you about how, moving along the riverbank, I never stop talking about the continuation of history. A motorboat, gasoline fumes, small, flat waves. Washed-off troddenness is continuation uncoiled from the spindle of no beginning. Unhurriedly to scatter and gather the smalt of the question expressed in the sentence "what is history?"

The hysterization of the event's body. An assumption: the sequence of an acting, idle, involved, or, if you like, participating person's reactions to extinction and emergence—noise is extinguished and, at the same instant, emerging from an entirely different source in a set of new sounds, waves, irritations of the membrane that excite imagination. A second is not a measure of time. How is "a second" different from "three and half years"? Is the signified of "never", "letter", or simply "plane" subject to description? Stop those gestures of yours! We're talking to you, in plain human language. What were you doing on the roof? Who talked to you? Why? Stay calm, try to remember. You were walking down the street, right? Fine. You were walking down the street, and meanwhile... yes, meanwhile, a yacht sailed by... did you remember the time? No, I didn't remember the time. I remembered something else. This is exactly what we're after. Try to stay calm and remember what seemed to you *something else* at that moment. Is it really that important? Trust us, it's enormously important. No... I don't remember.

The quantity of consonants and vowels. What meaning is placed in the hollow shell of events? Yes, an onion undeniably consists of the same onion (the sting of an arrow is withdrawn from the custom of description, yet what matters in many projections is not the arrow's completion in its coming-to-naught, negation-bearing point but its vectorial growth); death consists of its presentiment, removed, layer by layer, in an approach to a word—any word that by definition can't be captured: every understanding turns out to be an attempt to imagine sense as a finite, completing number, a number that fulfills itself on the threshold of the number that follows. Let's assume that the time of the traveler is counted from the vertical, steel slab of point C. The war will end, and birds will sing. All along the old, broken highway. Marcel, we'll meet in Pannaquin, over a cup of chocolate; we'll sit there, lost in the snows and the paths of bird migrations, entwined by vines in the emerald snows of swirling pages, among the tracer rustle of mountain bike tires, weightless like the breath of Aeolus, on the edge of the Universe, where closing your wind-burnt eyes, you see Europe, the Mediterranean, archipelagos with names countless like the treasures of moments growing in crystals—you see it all for real as the address of interruption. A swarm of stopped dreams. The gaze draws into the (perceptibly humiliating) recognition procedures the signifier of the plane on which someone of an indeterminate (apparently, because considerably remote) age and gender sets out on the road, that is, on his way—into snowstorms, heat, danger, open doors behind which there they are—I'll say!—because they already know how it'll all happen, and I don't. Instead, I get the following phrase: "the weight of time equals the weight of a wristwatch minus the weight of the bracelet of fake gold." It's dear to memory. I won't have the time before I die. I'd be happy if it wasn't for this cheerless autumn wind. Part by part, incredibly slowly, perpetually in doubt, we return what the world has given us at birth. Perhaps this is the eternal return that dissects *presence* into the eternal non-coincidence of "I was already" and "I will be again." Metabolism of illusion. A circular beating: substance departing the given. One should have tried to capture the thinnest rupture of duration, or a fly. From the days of early youth, I was fascinated by the lie of continuity. And now I imagine that I *remember* myself in youth. The main task is not to disclose continuation. We get history this way, or a set of objects that comprise it. Each of them—if anyone ever came to its end—twinkles with a possible knowledge; the ghostliness of this knowledge doesn't dishearten. The growing noise conceals all thinkable shades and overtones of true sound. Truth resides/rises in noise, changing the substance of its perception—becoming the noise that conceals the truth of indefatigable erosion, unraveling, and foliation: the growth of erasure. Of garbage. You, obviously, know nothing. It couldn't be otherwise. But who knows whose way the tide of tidings is headed, only to leave a permanent layer of karst in blood vessels? There is no interpretation. You read it the way it reads you. Between you and speech there is language. Charon as a communicative function. And it's of no particular interest. Petrified heaps of garbage. The ocean gives it generously and unconditionally. The ocean is irreproachable, like the formula of the refraction of light in Lautréamont's anthracite prisms. The crystalline temples of stone. The eye's pupil is insatiable in bad weather. When one returns to "PERSONAL WRITING". After that, there is the pulsation of the ellipse. The archeological layer of the message. The history of "O". No, it's all different; all she says is said by someone else. For excessive distribution in space there is parataxis. And who were they, may I ask? Ventriloquists? Demons? Children? Leaves, dry like the shells of events? No, what demons—they were ordinary psychotherapists. I command myself (to be sure, in the same friendly tone of voice!): "you don't drink; you never drank; it's someone else's life, not yours, that clings to alcohol, chemical whirlwinds boiling at the concave bottom of the grape; you are just a simple child in a cambric shirt, sitting on the window sill of a dirty house where you dream that you're the chaste letter 'O', the gold hoop of imaginary growth, the calendar distortion of heavenly bodies' course, or the pattern of birthmarks on your mother's back—remember those birthmarks on which father once told your fortune, like on Wharf-Khlebnikov's verbal tablets?" Thus each sentence could have been written by someone or something else. By rain. By dust. When there's much of it, and it's unsettled. And then?

The melancholy of visual culture throws reflections on the shoals of kites.

Ice, the melting of angels, victorious sounds of a trumpet on the drawbridge, heaps of road metal, archipelagos of dentures in the waters of many corrosions, hazy screams of seagulls, a few words, now finally incomprehensible—such is the remainder with which we'll have to spend the rest of our lives. Of course, this seems sad. To smile with false enthusiasm, to shrug one's shoulders (who would've thought!). To add: a staircase, weightless, slanting light on someone's face, struggle on the stairs. To add the unpredictable constancy and persistence with which death is given substance.

Even the most transparent strand of discernment is burdensome. There are no names. The affirmation "no" completely permeates experience. *Exoskeleton*. The underlying cause of history: "the body is a never-ending disavowal of itself as of something external." Or a distancing from itself that doesn't allow one to see who exactly moves along the plain. Each part, each fragment, or fraction is merely a bodiless, meaningless sign of an increase in the speed of forestalling the "whole." When a body falls in the bathroom, it expels a foamy stream of blood. The causes are unclear. The loneliness of soap is the last instance in the hierarchy of the unpronounceable, erased by what erases. We melt simultaneously, cherishing entirely useless snapshots of landscapes. Soul is nothing but a drawing of pores in their detailed transposition on rice paper. The sky consists of vowels and consonants, of common nouns, threads, and subsequent re-nunciation corrected by language. Telephones and shotguns (continue yourself)—the voice of thunder, the ear of water, the hand of lightning. Mythological prosthetics. Death drives its herds across a rather pleasant locale. Lilies, asphodels, asphalt. Do you recognize it? She's on the left in the photograph, and it seems, there, between the two heads completely faded from point-blank shots, is me... What does "it seems" mean? No, I don't remember. You've got to be in it too! Finally, there are objective proofs. This is my criticism. It needs to be taken into account next time we return to the narrative. We also need to make a few changes. And in addition, we need to provide a footnote for the sentence *"slipping on a soap sud, the protagonist... fell in the bathtub and ~~split his skull~~ (sic!), broke his head on the edge of a metal medicine cabinet"* because, despite obvious similarity, the author's reminiscence invokes not the death of Marat, but a domestic thriller about a leader of a liberation movement who fell victim to an insidious betrayal by his associates in the course of party struggle; as a result, on a cold autumn day he was killed amidst vases with asters chaotically placed all over the house (in the bathroom itself asters gave way to bunches of dry chrysanthemums) by a housekeeper dressed in a crepe-de-chine, mustard-colored dress with an open back, who, pretending she needed something, entered the bathroom, and no doubt, had her intentions misinterpreted by the leader (sex, as we'll find out later, is a trivial projection of curiosity) floating in the cooling water in a boat of soap suds with the wet proofs of a victorious speech in his chilling, marble hands—the speech was to be methodically read to the parliament later that day, with the arguments brought down on the heads of the bewildered colleagues like shells of heavy artillery. The sentence about the rivers of corrosion and the melting of angels in the icy glass of similarity also refers to this place. What do we have in the end? JFK Airport? A poetry stage? A gun carriage and Chopin, through whom nothing is gained?

"I'll only stay a minute," said Fr. Lob, squeezing in sideways. "Have you heard? They compared the murder of Mr. G. to the murder of Marat, no less! Was shot with an AK in his own hallway. Dear Lord, I'm melting like a chunk of butter on a pan... I hope you listened to my advice and included an appropriate footnote to indicate the fallaciousness, and furthermore, naïveté of such an approach! This heat is unbearable, simply unbearable—who will tell me how I'm supposed to live in such weather?"

"I'm asking you, where do we live?" Fr. Lob asked suddenly, immediately giving an answer in someone else's voice, "A country of know-it-alls... a land of... the overeducated." The phone rang. The ring outsmarted me, reminding me it was time to make coffee. "I'm overcome by thoughts," continued Fr. Lob. "I'm not sure... I'm full of uncertainty about the future. If things continue this way, I'll have to wake up Karl. I can't leave him here, can I?" "Where do you think is *here*?" I asked mechanically, not at all thinking about Karl who existed in two flat lives simultaneously, as though drawn on the frozen glass of a bus with a fingernail, making no attempt to link them in one line—so as to be understood at least one hour a day. I also didn't think about why my imagination responded to the word "Karl" with the picture of a fragment of a frozen, caked mass, a raised spot of slag, which didn't correspond to my actual view of it as a mere object of a sentence either. "In that case," said Fr. Lob, "I'd resort to the now old-fashioned term 'meaning-image'—as a working concept, it'll stay in circulation for quite some time." Perhaps this is why I got sick of persistent thought requiring the resolution (let's say, unfettering— liberation from the fetters of the particular, if one were to follow the habitual impulse of querying the etymology of a trite assertion) of a certain, apriori given, dark, "intentional" spot, or simpler still, of a problem, or a task whose solution was as usual to become the next stage of the continued movement of recognition which ought—let's use comforting imagery—to sew together shreds of forming, still-becoming information into a whole of experience. On the phone they told me something I completely forgot in a few moments. Some remember what others understand, and still others want; others understand what some remember and still others want; still others, in turn, want what some remember and others understand. Somewhere in here. I was left with coffee and the pages in front of me, in which I was to find something noteworthy. That's out of the question, surely. This is what I believe. But how should I understand why, when reading the word "dikikh," my imagination quickly and smoothly "wove the image" of a person, a character, a man, while also thickening his nominal habitat into something understandable and familiar? The rain filled the trunks of beech trees with velvet ink, endowing the sky with the exquisite opaqueness of a badly translated book, a reading of which is sometimes spiced with the tasteless bitterness of spring.

We spent time on bridges, staring at running water. Fishing rods broke in reflections. The line, stretched slantwise, trembled as though the sad power of the wishful dead had been imparted to it. Nothing departed. "My youth is gone," he'd usually say, rolling up his sleeve to stretch his hand out across the entire table for the roast dish. The proper name "Dikikh" will later be changed to "Turetsky". Such will be our ruse. A short, trifling ruse, but better than nothing. Business was going badly. "Postcard poetry and assistance to beginning authors" have lost their appeal. In the country where I spent my life, everyone wanted to be a writer and became one. A matter of taste.

"It's not a matter of postcard poetry," Vera said once, pulling her shawl tighter.

"Indeed," I agreed.

"A young man wants us to look at his manuscript. He wants to turn it into... a novel, or perhaps a novella. It doesn't matter. I don't think I need to explain to you what it could mean to us."

"No, you don't need to explain."

"Good. The material won't take too much time. We'll look at it and send it to the printer."

"If I understand you correctly, he tried to write something, and nothing came out of it."

"It came out fine."

"And what will this young writer pay us—me, that is?"

"He's not a young writer. And he'll pay us. That is, he'll pay me, and I'll pay you."

We both knew the agency was in its last days.

We also realized that chance wouldn't change a thing, even if it came in the form of a Nabokov or a Berdyaev. And in general, nothing changes anything. It never did—most importantly. That's exactly what I told her:

"Vera, you smoke way too much! You reek of all the fires in history! And besides, you can see for yourself that our meeting with the young writer changes nothing. Suppose, I read his manuscript—just for your sake, of course... By the way, who knows—maybe it'll reveal something extraordinary indeed. But I repeat—you don't care, it's like being up against a brick wall—even if he does pay us a few pennies, nothing will change.

"You see," I said blowing a few deft smoke rings, "it's not a matter of the manuscript or the young man—and you know this better than me. I'm surprised by something else. It's inconceivable—I still can't imagine why you started this so-called *business*."

"Why are you only asking this today? Why weren't you worried about it before?"

"Because I never thought which side they'd be shooting us from when we leave the house."

"Now I'm beginning to see...," she said with a drawl.

"What are you beginning to see?"

"At the very least, I see why lately you've been refusing to have dinner with me!"

"If I'm not mistaken, last time I was asked out to dinner was four years ago, on the day of the first cherry blossoms!"

"Did cherries really blossom that day?" asked Fr. Lob suspiciously.

"What does it matter now?" I replied.

"It must have mattered then. And what about the manuscript?"

"What manuscript?"

"I don't understand—you said she'd given you a manuscript..."

"What do you mean?"

"I mean exactly this," Fr. Lob whispered in the café after a young man with a friendly smile inquired when his "notes" would be ready. The man who'd sat down at our table was wearing a light, pale, well-tailored suit. His tie was also pleasant. It was obvious this tie wasn't the only one in his wardrobe. His slightly bloodshot eyes indicated that either he spent his time on the beach or had started drinking early. I opted for the latter as I couldn't find any trace of suntan on his face. There weren't any, as there were no traces of interest, even though it rang in his voice.

"It depends," I said to him. "You see, we're now flooded with work. Are you an author who sent us a manuscript? Well, you must be patient."

"Fine," said the man giving me his hand. "I've lots of patience.

"Turetsky," he added. "I thought that if we were to work together, you should probably know my name. My last name is Turetsky."

Fr. Lob grabbed Turetsky's hand and shook it in the air.

"Of course we'll work together. Lobov, " he said. "Call me simply Lobov."

"Do you also work in the publishing house?" asked Turetsky.

"Sure, from its very first days. To the best of my abilities. In the correspondence department."

I tried to imagine what sort of literature I'd be reading. I failed. I couldn't. The café was filled with cigarette smoke. Because of the music, all customers, most of them artists, but also others, probably artists too, or perhaps not artists at all, talked much too loudly. The man sitting in the corner was not an artist, even though he was a philosopher. He understood a lot, without show-ing that he didn't have time to understand all that he had once decided to understand. He ran about with lectures from morning till night, and worked as a marker in a billiard club near St. Nicholas Cathedral at night.

"Hi," he said, when I left the new acquaintance. "Sit down. How are things?"

"Well, well," I said. "A faun at midday repose."

"I got fired," he said. " But it doesn't matter."

"That's bad."

"Not really."

"What matters then?"

"Different things. You, for example, stopped developing the theme of dreams and carpets."

"For god's sake, who needs them?"

"You're mistaken. Everyone needs carpets. You, for example, need them for the meaning of the secret, not for what you think you need them for. If only there were carpets...," he grinned. "I just wanted to remind you, in a word. Do you believe me? Tell me you believe me, and I'll let you go."

"Today it'll cost you a lot more. It'll cost you two beers."

But thought, and perhaps the desire of it, lately have refused to stand before (more precisely, to "create") either riddles, or various hidden pockets (gaps? cavities? pores?) that form the real, etc. Histories attacked me on all sides again, grown quite wild, comparable only to hordes of barbarians (according to a different source, like a can of worms) on their way to breaching the shabby borders of an empire living in arrogant ignorance—only yesterday it successfully directed stellar rotation and the combination of welfare's overtones. Tree bark, chilling. Only at fifty did I begin to write the way I wanted to write all my life. What are the features of such writing?

I want you to go insane as you read this.
"You used to want something else."
"I used to believe in the growth of crops, in Fate marching in a crowd of masked revelers, and in my power to control the formation of kidney stones."

It's best for everyone this way. Besides, I'd like to find you. I still remember your picture on the silver plate of dawn which broke the circuit of my brain with a blind discharge of insomnia.

I'm probably not thoughtful enough at the moment, yet *this* very thought itself suffices—it's idle, aimless, and doesn't require any confirmation, not only of its own existence but also of my presence (ah, I still continue to believe that its beginning lies within me); this lazy thought, devoid of any thirst for comprehension and capturing, that, in addition, painlessly rejects the "I" as a fact filled with fictive possibilities, brings together, without any effort and desire to reign at the moment of entering the unknown, that which I, taking advantage of the unscrupulousness in the choice of means by both the writer and reader, would call "the different". The ambivalence of "permanence/change" is so trivial in its tireless vacillation that people forget about it in their never-ending debates about the problem of man's presence in the environment which he himself creates and is tirelessly transformed by. Here we begin to see the necessity of direct speech and confessions of love. I know what you need—you want me to go insane! But what are we then to call love? Didn't I tell you that my attitude to you was strange? I can't hear you. Speak more clearly, please. I don't see why we can't accept hearing, therefore, as the main component of the problem with the broadcast. It must be the fog... interference. I wonder if you hear me. Which of the countless fractions of the time and space we inhabit is more open to this state—if what we mean by love is really a state? Is it outside us, waiting for its season, or is it unreeled from us, unreeling ourselves to naught with it?

Karl's silhouette. The outlines are perpetually dirty. As are his things. Once he said, "...the gap between the world and the body is narrowing down. This isn't what upsets; one can gradually get used to it. What upsets is the subsequent coincidence with the world."

Incidentally, the kites have disappeared from view—not that it matters; after all, I don't have to observe natural phenomena with reverence all my life. With my head in her lap. No? I don't know. Speaking about "permanence" and "change" at some point means speaking about one and the same, or about two perspectives in which this "one-and-the-same" enters the game of consciousness and the countless acts contained therein, where one can't keep track of the weaving of permanent reality in its intention to comprehend the latter. In that case, I only need to remind you of the following: last time my confession occurred on the eve of your departure, yet I'd like to remind you that it's particulars of this very kind that have always been the weakest link in the chain, and sometimes it's incredibly hard for me to restore the past even when I need it to restore the present, which we either leave behind in our intentions or can't catch up with and from which we're swept away, tearing off all punctuational attachments, swept further away into indistinct mumbling where we imagine our times have their origin, because I'm not entirely sure that at this moment I sit at the table or in front of the monitor with a vague expression on my face, vainly trying to find in mutually erasing lines reasons for my reluctance (its trivial definition as a *particular sort of desire* is inescapable) to trust the authenticity of what's happening in actuality—in any event, I think you'll agree that back then we spent a lovely day and night in your (already unimaginably distant) house, granting that day and night, almost with a child's passion, the status of a beginning; the stream washes up on its fleshless border the pitiful remains of something you can't even find a name for—screams, whispers, dry seeds, laughter, peonies, a fence board warm to the touch, a plane tree, a drop doomed to an unaccomplished fall through sunny ripples, a drop of light or a drop of moisture that never reaches the bottom. In my later life there was less of this—things seemed to wane, thin out, preserving outlines and names—they resembled something like cenotaphs instead. I sometimes thought of Egypt—but in connection with something completely different.

But the courtyard, visible from the kitchen, delighted me as always with the ideal form of its sound, lagging in the gorge of emptiness, and with its complete indifference to everything, including sunlight that sometimes, on finding itself in the brackets of the courtyard's optional footnotes, changed nothing in the outline of what was in view and in its subtlest shades of typelessness—but on that day you brought me a bunch of jasmine and spent a long time trying to fit the flowers into a narrow green vase. I watched your skinny shoulder blades move under the hot silk of your dress; the strange difference between the temperature of the fabric and your skin kept bringing me back to the persistent thought that in the next world these beautiful, free-flowing dresses that unbutton so easily will apparently become the only reliable memory—I won't say more as I think about the losses incurred by significance when it's part of the comparison procedure, believing that an utterance is in itself a process of an exhausting, endless comparison, a game of equalizing a performance on the stage, yet it's hard to resist (writes he/she/it, breathing on fingers) responding to its temptation again, in an attempt to imagine myself telling you about that which I hastily tried to express a few lines above—I used to think (when?) that you might like the comparison of my (or, if you like, anyone else's) condition to an adaptation to the limits of the room in which you live, i.e., to its purest limits set by the redistribution of many things, objects, intersections of their echoes, perspectives, etc., each of which may be filled with the circulation of the only meaning you think important and true, and any of these meanings contains something that under certain circumstances could excite memory and imagination mixing, at elusive ratios, what will be with what has never been, and this something, at the same moment, won't fail to link with another object—an existing one or one irretrievably lost—in a word, to weave a cobweb of connections to anything at all (but how and for what purpose do these associative chains form?)—in other words, the surrounding world, that is, I, wanted to say in the kitchen back then, watching you fiddle with the flowers while the windowpane behind you picked out the enchanting courtyard, which radiated that particular grayish, mother-of-pearl Petersburg luminescence, burning to ashes any intention to extend light in the understanding/description of the fact that the "place" of my incessantly escaping being-there is created by simple things of this sort, by their correlation, while these very things become penetrable after some time for the gaze, body, mind, and turn into an invisible, wave-like non-event of a flame, existing in their hovering absence more convincingly and distinctly than in the first moments after one encounters them—but who remembers how they appeared, took their space, generating an aerial whiff of their own necessity or of their invasion (it's amazing, how often this delighted, brought real joy!), determining, in their constant absence, the borders of corporeality and its freedom, that once on a spring day, I inadvertently threw up my head amidst an approaching dusk on 5th Avenue near 46th Street and saw a shred of newspaper fluttering at the level of the 50th floor, ascending with a slow inevitability among walls and skies.

I slowed down and nearly stopped. I don't remember, there must have been someone else there. Remind me please. Now it's time to admire the moon. Like that woman on the metro, with a bag of live shrimp and a little volume of Wittgenstein in her lap. The uselessness of the shred of newspaper, its absolute needlessness, raised the garbage splash to the rank of a majestic parting with the habitual forms of former existence (two, three minutes, or forty-two years ago—the strain of identity in the obvious awareness of difference). I'll say this for myself, I won't listen to you. What has never been pronounced cannot be repeated. The space between consciousness and the body is left to culture and beads. The abandonment and desolation of childhood suddenly moved to a different dimension—was it time, space, expectation, premonition, reminiscence? This shift promised nothing, except the usual mistrust of what happened. The question, however, implied that "what happened" didn't seem to have happened because it was already present in experience as its own growing absence—it had already happened a long time before—no, it may have simply peeled off all of a sudden—that is, by itself, without any need for me. On the other hand, it would be a mistake not to consider the complexity of aerial jet patterns. The person with whom I was returning from some poetry reading—not entirely necessary for either him or myself—and who is no longer living, also looked up; his eyes were washed clean in a split second by the approaching evening.

If I'm not mistaken, he said, foreign cities grow incredibly large by the end of the day—they lose their beginning, but this doesn't last long—soon comes night.

So, he said, night comes along, and you don't know what to say, how to finish what you started saying, and for that reason everything starts over again at night. As soon as you start over again, you begin to realize that you're doomed to endless, empty pursuits, and you can never get to the end, even though the end doesn't exist, and you know that too. What exists is the newspaper flying upwards and we ourselves, carrying our bodies down the street, which explains, in part, why history has no end and is doomed to beginning. I didn't answer him, I was drunk. He too. We answered no one and watched the shred of newspaper being carried by wind to the still light skies of Times Square through which a sparkling airplane dragged a banner that said "...we're reduced to counting beads because our hands are too short to reach for the jug."

Existence is determined by the obliqueness of its "non-presence." It's more understandable this way. Much more understandable. This is impossible to read. To the same extent as it's impossible to write this. Once in the street, he said after a short pause, an unknown girl approached me with the question "do you write?"—meaning, apparently, whether I was writing at that time, that is, "whether I was working on a particular piece," as it was once customary to say. I looked at her as though at an idiot, obviously feeling quite awkward soon after. Among identical "impossibles" lies the only possibility: mine. Mine as such, without any objects or attributes. Things, if returned by fire, testify in various ways that they exist for nothing. That's the principal, primary, final lesson. But this exhortation is written in foul ink. What do the spots in front of you resemble? A house? A cloud in the shape of a piano? Money? Sexual experiences from childhood? A statue of Lao-tzu departing on bullback for the lands of sunset? Sexual organs of butterflies? The whisper of Scardanelli (the name that challenged the lines of many hymns) doubling the endless "yes" and disappearing in this doubling into the maternal tenderness of "no"? Who is standing by the tree? Should we trust freedom? The rain blurs everything—roads and hill slopes— it fulfills its duty not to interrupt the communication at any cost—the umbrella's silk top gets dark. The day gets dark. This is why one may say, putting out one's cigarette in an irreparably cracked cup with the remains of chocolate (raising oneself up, already reaching out for the books on the desk, already not here, but in the drizzle, on the beach, in the hallways one walks so easily, while still here, not quite straightened out yet, still raking up the coins with one hand, still...), "old age is antichronological". This is how history changes its nature in some endlessly becoming simultaneity. I remember how later, sitting in a bar on Bleeker

Street, we discoursed on the stress of getting used to new houses, where things are obvious, coarse, determined by the matter of their being and by their designation, but more importantly, by their position—hence to pick up a cup, one needs to find it somewhere on the map of the mental landscape, then find its analogue in real space, and only after that take it in hand with distrust, feeling a strange, slightly unpleasant surprise from touching the anticipation of form.

In Encinitas I dreamed of my father's funeral. The dream asserted, with all its unthinkably inappropriate bodily palpability that this funeral was to be the last one. The final one. Shifting from one foot to the other and stooping in the piercing wind, I indifferently recalled that I'd had plenty of these funerals in my life.

Some years went by without them at all, while in other years they took place almost every morning. We'd get up at dawn. Mother would put on a dress, prepared the day before especially for the occasion, and a wide-brimmed hat of "rice straw" with a little bunch of pansy pinned to the side of the crown; we'd then go hand in hand across the city to one of the cemeteries. Now I understand how a passerby must have felt on seeing us, for example, in January. But summer rewarded us a hundredfold—we got lost without a trace in the motley morning crowd.

I was standing in front of a pit dug out with an excavator bucket across a grading road (the latter both put me on guard and annoyed me with its impenetrable, malicious stupidity), while in front of me I saw the backs of people who were in turn looking intently ahead, i.e. in front of them. What is this, I'd think, breathless with rage, until when and how many times is this going to happen? What are the guarantees that this funeral is final? Who will give me these guarantees? Not that it was too exhausting—something else was the matter: the after-taste of some hopeless hackwork.

The dream's unfolding narrative gradually made it apparent that father was being buried for the hundred-and-seventeenth time. This time the weather was gloomy, dry, and slightly frosty. At the same moment, when the number asserted itself in the guise of a straw wisp (with which rye stacks are tied), I felt the touch of gray ice on my eyelids. "Who will vouch that this is the last time?" I heard a voice that, on sober reflection, could only be mine. Feeling the insufficiency of every breath, not moving an inch, I read, as though addressing my father, a short eulogy prepared long in advance; its content got a bit outdated by the time I uttered it, but I didn't hear my own words because of burning wind gusts—at the same time, I could read on my lips the words that, piece by piece, with an inexplicable crunch, were leaving my mouth where my teeth crumbled in the cosmic cold. Hoarfrost fell from the sky. Through the rime hanging in the air I discerned, on dry tree branches, a few black ravens instead of the usual Russian crows; the still helpless cold blossomed around them in motionless turbulence. It must have been unbearably stuffy in the metallic, endless luminescence of the day hidden in the oily folds of the dream. Returning to what was said above, I'd like simply to point out that these days things have become twice as penetrable—I often hesitate in front of an object, sometimes experiencing a hardly describable bewilderment, or at times fear, because these objects lose their habitual resistance that throughout my life kept me away from that which, according to the hints of my unfading suspicion, was lying behind the wall. But even there—if we're destined to cross over to that place sooner or later—how will we recognize each other? There'll be neither similarities, nor differences. Some time ago I read a few pages from my own book published not too long before—and in just the same way recognized nothing from what appeared before my eyes. They seemed to have wanted something else (repetition?). I couldn't quite understand what exactly. It seemed that in the shreds of their conversations, in some strange way addressed to me, one could sometimes guess some meaning, and indeed, there were moments when I was just about to agree with them entirely and share their joy or... perhaps, sadness (I can be mistaken), when after a while I slipped into the whirlpool of unintelligibility again. Their patience was boundless. The sun rises, one of them would utter distinctly. People deserve a better fate, another would continue. A dark-faced, attractive woman (an amethyst ring, thin fingers) sitting further away by the door more often than others turned to the idea of human destiny and the secret destiny of a chosen nation. I repeat, I wanted to agree with them in everything—does anyone know how much I need agreement, even if of a hasty kind?—although I was puzzled at the same time why indeed man deserves a better fate, why some nation must be chosen—more importantly by whom?—while its "secret" destiny called up in my imagination the strange image of a huge, unfamiliar building with broken windows, the black dough of a motionless mob down below, and a cold star trembling like a green needle in the viscous air of tender affection and mean hatred. But they didn't seem to notice me any longer when I, following them, also tried to tell some story—for example about jasmine, about rain hiding in the bushes, about a courtyard divided by a board fence in two halves, or about the deep, black moon of a well, breathing the fresh fragrance of nocturnal flowers and petunias. They nodded, pretending that it undoubtedly meant a lot to them, but after a short while, they interrupted me again with absurd questions even though I, partially out of spite, continued my stories. I said, you're finally done with the flowers. The gilding on the upper lip of the vase has peeled off in places and was scaling. A tiny leaf of something like glass or scales faded away on your finger, reflecting Petersburg's cool, sunken sky, a house across from us looking down at the waters of the Ebro, the expanse of the street finely inscribed in the nocturnal murmur coming only from the following source: in the convex mirror of measured comparison with blooming roses of smoke behind its curtains, a few people conferred in muffled voices about the necessity of investigating the death of the charioteer. You liked to sit on the window sill facing the room, with your legs spread and resting on the radiator; you wanted me to embrace you and someone else (if this someone was lucky enough) to see your skinny, naked back, vertebrae, and the arms embracing you. And, as you'd say, they're sitting there, far away, at the very end of the corridors of magic glass, in the rooms where wind probably wanders, stumbling over corners, and where they drink wine, indulge in mesmerizing calculations (a rather good example of how distorting optics work), lament the death of a run-over goldfinch, or simply sit in a stupor because everything is over, including the day, and notice me, sitting on the window-sill of the fourth floor, while in addition, the street below never gets quieter—yet another stream of cars turns in from Liteiny—at first they think I'm embracing myself, and only after a while would one of them break the silence and say, look how long her arms are—arms can't be this long, you can't embrace yourself this way..., and then, staring at me, undressing me further (though I already have nothing on—you took it all off when you talked about silk dresses, remember?...), they'd understand that the arms behind my back aren't my own, while our barely perceptible movements (this is why I asked you to be discreet), their particularly unobtrusive rhythm (you can strike this off) testify to something other than her—that is, *my*—desire to attract attention. The logic of such copulations is unpredictable; it isn't altogether inelegant at times and for that reason gives pleasure. No matter what the coupling is like, at this moment it is surely no less true than false. The smell of jasmine comes from below. Many died, but many managed to hide in the mountains or self-description.

Once on a train, on the way back from Moscow, in the dusk of afternoon slumber wandering along the unbending line of the train's movement, I caught my imagination at a painstaking and rather strange job: it methodically and measuredly wove your death. The details came by themselves, booming and empty; their purpose was perhaps to divide and distribute space without communicating anything about time, place, and on what grounds they addressed you. In the cold, vertical planes of the crowded street, I rigorously singled out (an imperfection of short-term memory) fragments of curved, colored spots and your image filled with the sweet speed of their every fall, as though floating in stagnant waters.

Draughts determined the direction of cool air.

Speech consisted entirely of prepositions. A few points.

In one of them we're beautiful. In another, eagles get covered with ice and exchange etched-through coins of heaviness with air. In the same point where we're beautiful, there are a few books. Their content is known to everyone, but no one is able to retell it.

You walked against the sunset shade along the wall of Kazan Cathedral, and further on, just like in the letter: she crossed Kazanskaya Street, took a few steps in the crowd of a trolley bus stop, got pushed by that crowd to the wall of a building where there once was a Georgian restaurant; meanwhile the crowd was limply pushed back towards the arriving trolley bus, and she, pausing to wait out the spasm of its chaotic movement, mechanically took another step back, finding herself across from a phone booth (in those days, such booths were everywhere); its iron door swung open noiselessly—as though with some unstuck sound—like a shadow from a fish tank, sliding in the outside towards the door of the trolley bus that closed just as slowly (but for entirely different reasons); you were close to the point where one sees nothing at all, however, you were already carried downstream by the hot garbage wind, in the riverbed of a waterless, flat plateau with its rock heated to the state of transparent mica and its blood depleting into boiling molecules of thirst, turning "always" into "never", showing the eye regions of eternal wind, of a rumble torn on edges, and of lacking details. The sphere of investigation narrowed down.

"I think I even saw this in that dream, though there's a clear temporal non-coincidence here; there should be no coincidence, at any rate. But I think that when I felt the snake bite, I immediately began to see a lot of things at once: I saw, for example, my hand and yourself in the place you just described—waterless rivers, some riverbeds crossing red plateaus, black pine forests, and the wind—its icy blankets of snow, unusual for the parts where I happened to be, seemed a horrible heat wave pulling me with each turn out of my words and body. I seemed to see you in the crowd; if I'm not mistaken, your voice didn't stand out in the chorus—you stood like children stand in front of a camera (I remember those drops of sweat flowing down your face as though I were a video camera) and looked at the wall of the very building we visited one morning. But what's the name of that place? Where did it happen? What's the name of the river in which your head will float? How do I know about the river? Where did you fall behind? Where did everything change so quickly? What will your open eyes reflect? What will we get for it? Why did everything go so quickly?"

"Because we lived faster than others died," says Fr. Lob.

"I don't understand," says Turetsky with irritation. "OK. I read the description of the room a few times. Here... who, for example, is this woman he's talking about? Further, is she fictional or does she have a prototype?"

"I don't recall one."

"Why don't you? He writes about how he looks out into the courtyard, and there's no one there because, as he writes, everyone seems to have gone to the country, to their dachas... What's with this tradition to write about dachas? Anyway, let's leave dachas alone—so, he stares into the courtyard, and a girl with flowers must be waiting for him in the room. It's her that I'm asking about: who is she and why does he always go back to her in other places—even though, frankly, I don't think it's always the same girl. Do you think it could be his wife?"

"Well, why necessarily wife? Just... just a woman, that's all, a literary character. What exactly are you trying to get out of me?"

"Can I be honest with you?"

"Our relationship presumes nothing else."

"Then listen. First of all, I don't want him to edit my novel, and I'm most grateful to you—if it wasn't for you I'd still be in the dark... do you know what's important to me? It's important to me that the editor understood me at least partially. Do you agree?"

"Makes sense."

"And what *follows* from this?"

"As far as I can see, nothing *follows* from this," said Fr. Lob.

His face, calm for ages, was now clean and perfectly impeccable—beyond age and continuation—while his glasses reflected a sky of dark gold and also "his face, calm for ages and now clean in the sense that it reflected nothing." A thin-armed, swarthy tree and wild reeds grow from my friend's eyes now; there's nothing he can do, save avoid restless flashes gliding on the glass of his spectacles—covering them with his hand, withdrawing, becoming all invulnerability, fatigue, old age, and other things of this sort, yet not the things that come to mind.

Nights in Petersburg are particularly cold this time of summer. The Atlantic changes the vector and measure of its breath. The islands in the delta blacken sharply. Sometimes snow falls by night. I tell him about it. I remind him of the years when snow fell in June and stayed on the cooling poplars. In the first person.

"Well, others have grass growing in their streets," he says, suppressing a yawn. "Hot-cold. What does it matter? Ah, my dear friend, don't rush the night! Why don't we smoke a cigarette? Why don't we have some wine before we smoke a cigarette? And why don't we go see some ladies after we've done both these things?" He falls silent for a while. Then he adds,

"It appears I'm exposed to be consumed by the future, i.e., to become a laughing-stock. My past," he says, "is now no more than a sticker with woodcutters, Puss in Boots, Tom Thumb—a picture that you lick and then paste anywhere. It's criminal to think that many years ago I didn't imagine myself in this very way, sitting on the edge of fuck knows what, knowing quite well *how* I'll be telling someone about the fact that in some past I supposedly already knew the past would never happen, never would be. But in old age, even the most stubborn people try to palm off names back on things, not on names—if there was an authority keeping constant track of such loans, then this authority would be the reproaching finger that one's free to take for anything at all. And the logic is clear and simple. It's banal. They're not content with the possession of names—and they indeed entered into possession of names from the very beginning; they inherited this right. It's important for them to become convinced that all this was created precisely to belong to them. Only Karl realized how utterly ridiculous it is! No one owes anything to anyone. No names. Death offers the only chance to completely immerse oneself in pure, non-becoming relations, to become a laughing-stock. And those fingers as though made of warm plasticine. Did you ever happen to shake hands with such a person? Disgusting."

Chirping like an insect, the camera snatches close-ups of sweat drops on a wrinkled face. The film theater was housed in a long, rebuilt shed for agricultural machinery. It gradually acquired additions, and when I started seventh grade, there was even a soda stand. There's more color in black-and-white films than in color ones. The game of pebbles was for money. To make a film about a city, about doors, window frames, and rusty iron of unknown purpose is a rewarding task. There are roofs, poets, fingernails. Memories of the war alternated with discourses about possible changes. The epic character and hypnotism of the former and the petty helplessness of the latter. History lacks a primary source. Various things, many fairy tales. It sometimes failed to happen. As the first condition of any narrative. It happened nonetheless.

Yet I prefer phloxes, and when there are none (which happens sometimes), gillyflowers. Did my birth (this time I mean my physical appearance in the world) presuppose more than a separately existing fact, available today thanks to a little-substantiated oral narrative? I'm not even sure that the person born was "I". My mother seemed to have similar doubts. She seemed to suspect (particularly in her last years) that my existence owed more to the neighbors' stories than to objective biological or historical facts. Who knows, maybe the neighbors indeed wanted something from her—I wonder what exactly. To be included in her will? Alas, she had nothing to will. She had given away all her jewels (my favorite earrings with sapphires were among them) to graveyard beggars a long time before; in gratitude, they relieved her from the dream that had haunted her for several years—the dream of an open inkwell falling from a desk onto the floor. "Just imagine how painful it is: you reach out to dip your pen in the ink, and the bottle starts to list slowly, as though getting caught in a stream of glue, but nothing can hold it on the edge… And I fail to finish my letter—but the most awful thing is that when I see it falling again and again, I completely forget what it is I wanted to write; I'm left only with the vague and bitter sense that what didn't get written was extremely important. And then, where did that confounded bottle come from? Remember, we never kept any inkbottles in the house. Well yes, if I was completely naïve, I'd certainly believe that death itself tried to prevent me from saying something that could keep it from me for good, but to tell you frankly, I think I'm actually quite happy that everything goes, gets forgotten. Because it must all go without a trace before I'm no more. Otherwise, what's it for?"

I still can't understand who wanted what. Meanwhile, the canned food that by some miracle had never run out ever since World War II was suddenly gone from the pantry. All her hats (how I missed the one of thin, violet velour—I remember her so young in Rostov-on-Don—the shadow of the hat brim falls on her face, but it looks even lighter and closer because of this; her gray eyes are full of tender laughter and radiance; and remember the quick turn of her head—she just heard something and is now trying to see it too—the turn doesn't take the recollection any further; remember those short pauses for breath before she laughs?), all those hats turned to dust, and every time someone thoughtlessly opened up the boxes, swarms of may-bugs would fly out. The bugs dried up, crunched underfoot. Nobody cleaned them out. Focused on the impossibility of taking the pen to the ink in her dream, she failed to notice how on a stormy May night the gold cookware at once became brass, heavy, and useless. "Promise me you won't rush to get married," she'd sometimes say to me, deep in her thoughts. "I see how you've changed, how much you like her, how you can think of nothing else. Strange, but your father most of all dreamed of the time when he'd meet your girlfriend—I know I'm being unfair to him. But I sometimes think that all my dreams about the ink bottle—thank God they're over now!—are about my wish to write a letter to your father…, and yet something about the whole thing must be wrong from the beginning."

Grandma's maxims annoyed her immensely. Grandma annoyed her also by her very appearance and, in part, by the fact that she met with some "shady" people who believed in the magic power of a sieve and apples tied together cross-wise with red threads. The apples were lowered into a well, and when it was time to draw some water, you'd pull up a bucket of both water and apples. That was the trick. As Grandma claimed, that way apples kept better till spring. "I can't believe it!" mother would exclaim, "you're a mature woman, you've lived a life, and just listen to your nonsense!" Of course, all that business with the apples and the sieve was a shameless lie, as was Grandma's story about an angel she saw on a plum tree from a fence (remember I told you about that incident?), but the shady people believed it without reservations—as they, in fact, believed her every word. But then why did I see her in two places at once?

"And how did you manage to be in two places at once?" asked Fr. Lob.

"I was in Kiev and saw her at the train station on my way back. That is, I saw her from the train window as she walked down the platform, stooping under some heavy sack. And in three hours, when I walked into the house, she was reading in the kitchen as if nothing had happened."

"Maybe she had a sister mother hadn't told you about."

"Quite possible," I agreed. "But what does it mean?"

I didn't want to say that I saw her one more time on the station platform in Kazatin, with the same sack.

This is simply outrageous! It's now been a week since they started stubbing those stumps. Amazing how time flies. Once mother couldn't help herself and asked a neighborhood locksmith to put Grandma on a chain. "And do you really think you've chained *me*?" said Grandma from the darkness of the room hung with drying herb bunches, "It isn't me you've chained—you've chained your son, and not to this trunk, but to sorrow." "Indeed," said mother, "if only I could, I'd drop this trunk of sorrow in the river, together with the bedbugs."

All fables of memory (some special, miraculous memory that supposedly captured in the "unconscious" the separation of my physical body from the maternal one) seem to me clearly exaggerated.

Guess, how old I am? Correct. But I accept my years with proper humility, no matter how many people there are in the room. Naturally, I can assume various things, including the ability of my memory to preserve details of this kind, but then another question arises: how can consciousness "become conscious" of them as its own? On the other hand, I'm not so sure it was I who spilled Villa Forest on my white pants. Dying in the participle. Dying in circular darkness. Speech isn't salvation, and it isn't plumage. I mean grammatical forms and autumn as a slow diversion into the tautology of the blank and the inferno of the palindrome.

When we talk about something, does it mean that we "think" about this *something* with something? That is, does speaking mean in this case a set of routine operations that keep on the same horizon a sensory image, meanings, senses, and sense links, including the still unapprehended logical structures of their further transformation into *something else*, which allows the functions of the fragmented to enter into the ghostly yet perfectly convincing relation of the general and the particular? No, probably not—if I hadn't decided to come see you then, in the pouring rain, everything would have happened differently. But, she says, there's something else here that surprises me: I distinctly remember leaving the house, riding in an empty tramcar—remember those rains, they started in the middle of July; nothing ever foreshadowed them, and that's how it was on that day—a remarkably bright, hot sky in the morning; you had just returned from the Crimea, and I really wanted to see you; you must have gotten one hell of a tan, I thought, while people here go crazy in their offices—but forgive me, I completely forgot how I got off the tramcar and how you looked when

I saw you—sometimes I think you simply weren't home, or... I got off sooner and decided to return home; maybe I remembered something about you, and it turned me back—you know how it happens... I think we often quarreled at the time... no, we didn't quarrel, but must have disagreed about something—I really don't remember what it was. Otherwise, why would we return to "certain subjects" countless times, sooner or later beginning to realize (and even then in passing, indirectly, as though unwilling to focus our thought on what was to reject it later) that every such repetition fundamentally crosses out, negates each preceding return/repetition. From which it follows (I agree, this turn of phrase is an entirely meaningless exercise in rhetoric!) that what I really need in an utterance isn't an otherness; what I need is to make every utterance senseless—and this for some vaguely manifested reason—to reduce everything said to an inarticulate residue, like an anticipation, murmur, indistinct subterranean boom (press your ear to the ground—you'll hear)—believing, besides, that "in language everything occurred ages ago". Then comes "yes, I understand". Understand what? Or could this statement be a conventional figure of restraint, implying "leave me alone, don't bother me with what doesn't concern you in the least"? Indeed, *understand* what? That to explain "the understood" one needs again to return to the utterance of what was already understood and by the same token exacts no repetition? Yes, you already spoke about this. I spoke about what? When? Are you out of your mind? I spoke about something else. About how one morning—sometimes (though less and less often...) there are such mornings in the fall when the surrounding world appears in quite different proportions and volumes, in different colors, and in durations of a different kind. Fog envelops half-bare linden trees, a slanting wall of October sun is quite obvious, and a giant, swirling rain cloud moves in from the northwest, covering half the sky, as though some celestial ranges have started to advance on the city—the slanting crest of the sun, tree leaves exhaling the light of tender plant decay, air filled with tart camphor, which gives the feeling that it's woven with icy strands of hoarfrost—let's call this "here".

We need "here" in order to understand "there"—or to put it differently, the correlation with what was called "there" (the dark tar color of thunderstorm sky and so on). The blind erection of a landscape in the dark is usually an uneasy task and requires substantial effort. Seeing the landscape also requires serious effort, because neither the leaf that touched your cheek in its broken, uneven fall, nor the atmospheric phenomena, nor the fragile equilibrium of the fog can separately become what they are in their totality—the moment of a prick-like, cold liberation from... say, truths. As a clarification I'll add that, if, for example, this morning I hadn't been released by hemorrhoids, I would've seen nothing; on the other hand, hemorrhoids with their persistent, secret presence in the suspended irritation of pain are undoubtedly also among the components of the landscape, on par with the decrepit system of memory that randomly offers "recollections," unthinkable in their lifelessness and laughable insignificance and supposedly bound to serve as the linking constituent of the perceived. Everything, indeed, every factor, including those that at a particular moment appear simply as pure, direct negations, in reality become an integral part of reality. In relation to them, many facts that possibly used to be quite significant are immediately found *outside* and *beyond*. Later these facts need to be extracted, brought back to life, or rather, implanted. Facts transplanted like organs. Same problems—rejection, incompatibility.

"And where have you read all this?" asked

Fr. Lob.

"On the way from Moscow to St. Petersburg, on a train," answered Turetsky evasively. "Lots of places where you can read it!"

"I don't understand how you can be moved by such ponderous nonsense!"

But I didn't let him finish.

"You've seen Karl, haven't you?"

"What of it, even if I have? *What*, do you think, I could've seen?"

A mirror on the left, a window on the right. Oh yes, even in nebulous childhood, whenever I asked mother about the deserted castle on the rock towering above the town, she'd press a finger to her lips and, looking pleadingly above my head, beg me in a barely audible voice not to tempt providence because, as it followed from her hasty yet always thoroughly repeated narrative, an extraordinary villain used to live there in ancient times; his greatest pleasure was to torture children and then eat them alive. A chastity belt puts certain ideas into your head. What sort of children? Bad ones? Children who keep their hands under the blanket at night? Children who've eaten the cake leftovers and are trying to hide it from God? No such luck. Like hell they will. This is how my dream to learn

Italian spread its wings. I'm thinking about the advantages of knowledge over ignorance, including the knowledge of Italian that could at least allow me not only to sing but also read Dante Alighieri in the original. Who the fuck needs him, your Dante.

Children in whose eyes the world's palest flowers blossom and whose bodies are bound by chronic sniffles. Children who in their feverish, muddy fantasies undress—maniacally, each night... the incomparable pleasure, like the Italian language, or language as such—the music teacher who came from the capital recently and lives across the street, two houses further up the road, towards the square; they sometimes do it extremely slowly, and at times frantically fast, yet still unable to complete the smallest bit, the last phase, cross the final line; thus nothing ever changes—one wonders only what to do with her *next*. Residue. Because it's a very real dead end, the worst hopelessness that could ever happen in dreams; it's also a genuine, endless crisis of impotence! No, such children indeed deserve to be eaten alive. No question about it.

Simply children. Children were most probably

getting transformed into some abstract material; in the end, the transformation wasn't so clear. In what way? Why? I looked at the rock, the castle and, turning away from my own image and body that until then had relentlessly followed on my heels like two wandering reflection axes, tried to understand how the existence of "children" could exist outside any status attached to their actions or functions. Is it altogether possible? Where would we then find what they call the wisdom of an infant (like the inborn ability to swim that we lose in the blink of an eye when we find ourselves by the ocean, for the first time discovering that we're ringed by our own bodies)? Childhood as the purest non-relational function (of the order of amalgam) was a desirable reward for him who saw it as an operator of doubling, multiplication, and tracelessness. I said to mother I was beginning to understand the motives of the villain who at one point lived in the castle on the rock reigning in the perforated letter of its span over the area. "Is that so?" she asked me, peering searchingly through her pince-nez into the ultramarine abyss of my eyes.

I passed my hand over my face, as if wishing to free it from an invisible spider web—this gesture, picked up from some book I read (the second book-case, third shelf from the top, apricots behind the window, the fingernail hitches up the silk of the bubbling curtain embroidered with wild poppies and blue-bonnets; my head after bathing is as though enclosed in an ochre-painted clay shell—two attributes are obviously superfluous), seemed to me both majestic, giving the necessary weight in the eyes of the audience, and expressing the extraordinary loneliness of the child's delicate soul. They gave me little money. I had to resort to stealing in the locker room of the rowing club—wasn't too hard as I mostly sat by myself on a raft, still learning the skill of paddle-handling. Only later did I get a Hedgehog; the vessel was an antique, but I was enormously proud of it and paddled it across the water with genuine elegance—the kayak seemed to change something in me, becoming the best part of my soul. The ownership of the light boat not only changed my metaphysical perception of the world, but also the world itself: I suddenly discovered I could understand the language of animals, birds, certain kinds of insects (not all of them, though), could hear the grass grow, and what the dead quietly talked about underfoot. Once, walking on the jetty to the exit with the Hedgehog on my shoulder, I, despite my constantly strengthening habit of self-absorption and self-analysis, listened hard and picked up some indistinct sputter and sighs coming from a dark corner; the sputter was first interspersed with exclamations, then there was a short silence, a suspicious noise, and finally someone's strange yet familiar voice continued its displeased muttering, as though begging someone about something—this is how half-awakened pigeons peck through the muslin of morning silence with their constant, fruitless complaints. When I came closer, I immediately realized that my comparison of what I saw to pigeons was extremely strained. Gibbon (he ravenously paddled a canoe and ate flies on a bet) was hauling up Zoya, a food stand vendor from the neighboring beach, by the rope with a noose on her neck (inconceivable how he'd managed to put it there!), that he'd thrown over a beam.

"I'm convinced that in such cases you get what you need with promises," said Turetsky.

"I wish," barked out Fr. Lob. "It doesn't always happen this way. He must have fed her some lies. I'm sure lies are a more universal approach than all sorts of promises."

"But can't a promise be false?"

"Psychologically, a promise is often self-sufficient."

"I won her from Shnift at cards," said Gibbon, squinting his red eye and exhaling desert heat. "You can try your luck—they're playing behind the jetty."

And he concluded:

"I wish I could see you in my place!"

There was nothing left to me but shrug my shoulders in response.

Everything was happening with an absurd neatness, almost mechanically. Gibbon would pull the rope, the girl would wheeze, Gibbon would mutter inarticulate swearwords, wait for a second or two, then let go of the rope; Zoya would nearly go underwater, and Gibbon would throw himself on her like a lion and start taking off her underwear, but Zoya would get over her swoon, open her eyes, give a tortured moan, and fight back with a force unexpected for her delicate build; yet Gibbon would again run headlong for his end of the rope, start pulling again, and everything would get repeated—I felt my mind was at its limit, I was slowly going mad. Tortoises, Sisyphuses, Achilleses turned their carousel, frantically rushing after each other, as though in a round dance on a red pelike. "Gibbon," I turned to him, opening my cigarette case and offering him a smoke. "Gibbon," I repeated, lighting up my cigarette and exhaling the slightly bitter smoke of my favorite tobacco. I was wearing white flannel pants, a beige sweater under which that day I had on a purple silk shirt;

my feet were clad in suede shoes with string soles. Wind gently played with my hair.

"Reality, my dear Gibbon, appears—but accept my sincere gratitude for the empirical opportunity you offered me to convince myself of the authenticity of what I'm about to say... No—and it's your right to reproach me for my inaccuracy—reality doesn't *appear*, but arises from the 'real' as a consequence of a certain feeling that it's possible—I *emphasize*—to lose that reality. In short, reality doesn't exist until the moment it begins to disappear, but you also can't claim that it, reality, exists in non-existence, and if it arises in the process of its own decay, then it inevitably passes over into the category of actuality, because we perceive it through our awareness of its very acts, i.e., of actuality."

Something else flashed through my mind about martins and lime leaf tea, but I felt I was inescapably losing interest in the idea that was previously so enticing. I had a tickle in my throat. My work wasn't done. There was very little time, and I had barely started. But the first sentence with which I wanted to start my review of the book *Colder Than Ice, Harder Than Diamonds* for *Kommersant Daily* had been prepared by fate a long time before.

The rest, as usual, posed no difficulty: "because

today the book has become nothing but a ritual text: from its very first pages (no matter what the title) the reader is invited to penetrate the 'eye of the cyclone' because it's there (where? what nonsense!) that reading is possible as an exceptionally powerful partition and dismemberment.

First of all, let us note that the author's perspective has nothing to do with evil. Indeed, our cosmos functions as/and human (anthropological extrapolations are removed) [...] although the plot, the anecdote itself seems too plain to be convincing. The book opens with a scene in which on the last Sunday in August someone hastily writes a review (the review has been commissioned by a well-known paper) of a novel that starts with an unremarkable description of an early morning in an apartment that bears obvious traces of excessive drinking the night before. The beginnings of the stories are unknown to the reader. It is also unknown how many of them have begun. One could surmise that some of those present played and continue to play the role of passive listeners, allocated to them by the author, which makes guessing the real narrators quite important. On top of it all, one begins to suspect that the stories in their subsequent exposition turn out to be different from the ones told the night before. For example, one of them, as it follows from the conversations coming from the kitchen where coffee is being prepared, started with the narrative of kite-flying in a small English town. Alas, the mention alone proves quite insufficient—the imagination only just begins to blissfully melt on the edges of dark brick, ivy, smells of coal burning in the fireplace, and so on (the reviewer is undoubtedly aware of how unnecessary he is in his rhetoric) when the reader begins to realize that something else is at issue here, which may very well be some pretext for the memoirs of the Wolf Man—or, rather, a certain idea for a hoax that occurs to a well-known Russian author of the period, hoax guaranteed to be used in time by certain circles to penetrate European financial markets. In passing, we find a fascinating description of Russian artistic life in Odessa where the literary cream of Moscow and St. Petersburg flock to in summer. One of the guests (his name is a little suspicious)—Associate Professor Lobov, if memory serves—makes a reservation, "I'm not sure that Pankeev would fail to meet W. …" Everyone pretends not to have heard these words. Pankeev himself manages a forced smile. He is pitiful. We will learn the reason for his smile later. In other words, the proposition made to him on the 11th Line of Vasilyevsky Island was not the first one. In addition, it becomes clear that neither the beginning of this particular story, nor its fake continuation in our reading (the novel itself) can be considered separately. Meanwhile, the reader, and we along with him, understand that we face a different, albeit again very simple order of narration—from the end to the beginning—despite the fact that the intersection point of the fictional *reverse continuation* and the actual development of the story to its future denouement is at first impossible to recognize as the beginning (constant beginning?) of another possible story having nothing to do with either the morning apartment, or with the company that wakes up there. As one imagines later, a significant although inconspicuous detail will make it easier to understand the existing circumstances, but even the awareness that the novel is set in a city where a war has been on (for 15, 30, 40 years?), only increases the confusion, adding an aftertaste of banality to the narrative; a 'turn' for a desert island would seem inevitable, if it were not for the phone ring and the overheard conversation (it doesn't matter, you should have called in the morning, because he's leaving; he did choose the episode with the phone booth—he liked it a lot and said that if he'd known sooner, he would have had a different attitude to actors' auditions—there's this actress here—to tell you the truth, she did fine, but something still lacked in her performance—it's a shame, sure—ok, don't waste your money, I'll let you go, give me a call as soon as you get back), while to anyone who wants to penetrate the novel in its life-size dimensions, we can only advise that they resort to questions of a metaphysical kind, because the amorphous and lyrical narrative burdened with irrelevant irony in the long run reveals hidden bifurcations of the plot, and not even so much of the plot itself as of the possibilities of such bifurcation. But what's really unexpected is the solicitous, if not downright reverential recourse to the tradition of detailed character portrayal, which in the future—if the author remains true to himself—promises to become, as they say, a 'grand style,' something many authors lack these days. This, in fact, is the author's first book. Until now, he has been known entirely by his all too scant journal publications; the edition is surprisingly tasteful, it is printed on nice paper, with a timid, yet somewhat arrogant print run; it ~~on the face of it, offers~~ leaves no possibility for mental projects of either the authors' friends, or of the author's very world... *I don't like your suicide at the end of the script; it's all so tasteless that, believe me, I simply feel sorry for you...* which today seems particularly incongruous and old-fashioned; at the same time, his classically sequential writing works, without carrying one off into faraway times, as a postcard mailed on an unknown date from an unknown place by an unknown correspondent of a lost scene/time of action..." Fr. Lob took his eyes away from the pages in front of him and thought, "to all things there is a season." Too bad, he thought, the evening promised to be nice and easy, like the lives of remarkable people.

But the familiar nausea was rising to the heart. It meant one thing: no matter what choice he made, the nausea would stay—like an autumn headache (perhaps this is what they call migraine, or at least, gout, or simply my life). Fr. Lob felt he was beginning to get slightly out of breath, yet the hope of a cure by wine wasn't particularly strong.

He saw, as if through a glass, his friends talking, snow drifting (you thought melting? of course not) in the lilac absence, and the brighter the light of underground lamps, the less distinct that which grows out of the dusk. Walking down Furshtadtskaya, Fr. Lob stopped a few times, as if afraid to scare something away with the sound of his footsteps—something that promised to appear to him, foreshadowed by an asthmatic fit that happened to him in a café.

He crossed the square by the circus but after some thought, turned back to Liteiny Prospect. Both the café and the friends' conversation were suddenly in an indefinite, not quite remote past. And to remember the present, thought Fr. Lob, is an entirely senseless business. It's enough to say that the expression "to remember the present" is quite meaningless already. And to remember the past is impossible because in the very ~~remembrance~~ (in the act of remembrance), its past turns into an illusory present, and the present needs altogether no remembrance of itself. Dragomoshchenko is wrong, he said out loud. On the other hand, I can't be present "here," I always seem to be stealing up to the past from "behind," from the past that already happened—any thought behaves this way. Still, how much I hate these... residents with their dogs at night—he deliberately got himself distracted and again hastened his pace, escaping the ghost of an answer. He was the first to whom the work of his brain resembled some reflection activity: stimulus—response (a pendulum). What decades ago used to cause almost dizziness, increased palpitation, complex anticipations, now became irrevocably different. It started long before Karl's first disappearance though. He vividly saw that day in the slow movement of various objects, in the patches of light from which Karl, leaning slightly forward, stepped out, sank down in a chair by the table, twiddled a book, and quietly said, "Lobov, I'm out of luck. I'm out luck for thinking I was really lucky. I should have thought it was all nonsense, and never returned to it again." What Karl told him could have been an utter lie, but unfortunately, it was all true. It was truth, plain and simple. Even a child could understand it. Karl could read everything on computer drives the way one reads a newspaper. He could also read what there "was" in the random-access memory at any given moment. He saw it in his own, unique way, but was then able to translate what he saw into sign systems available to him. Translation would later prove to be the weakest point. "You know, I see and understand everything, but how can I convey it all?" He simply described pictures with a limited number of modifications: there's a forest, a river behind it, a naked broad on the riverbank, and so on. The picture was opened, he put the money in his inside pocket. The strangest things happened in virtual reality. It was those things that one understood the least. His dynamic environment in principle couldn't be reduced to a disposition of data and their structure (an analogy with a virus), but only to the data's interaction with the perceiving subject, and so on. Then Karl disappeared. It was no secret who was interested in him. He himself knew that much was disappearing in front of his eyes, his very eyes—simply disappearing, that's all. And that their carefree and well-off life was coming to an end. A few days before his disappearance he dropped by at Yu.'s who two months later was put away for the rest of his life for supposedly breaking into the computer system of Wells Fargo Bank, left him some money—just in case—which Yu. passed on to Lobov that same night; apart from the money, there was also a notebook in the envelope; even after a very careful reading of the handwritten notes Lobov couldn't make any sense of them.

Of course, everything became different. Including love, muttered Lobov without taking his eyes from the roof line, "including love"—can't think of anything better. On the other hand, all spatial categories are irrelevant for meaning in the description of what occupies me at this moment: the present is the constant agony of absence, he began again, in a seemingly disinterested and humdrum tone, absent-mindedly stirring his fingers in the air, having established for himself that gesticulation peculiar to such a moment must be inexpressive, dull, that in the final analysis, one could easily make do merely with a grimace of slight bewilderment caused by the irrelevance of the grimace itself—it's more accurate to describe it like this: the agony of establishing non-identity. Actually, absence also never comes to pass; my time (or myself) is the rapture of time as such, non-being threatening itself with negation. This is how you find yourself before this rapture like a Narcissus unable to cross the line that separates him from himself. Further, there were passages about evening light and morning snow in New York, there were other images tied together by piercing cold, detachment, and simultaneously, a strange necessity to exist. One could describe them as aimless and therefore endless. One couldn't exchange them for any memory, but their doubtless power caused a fragile sense of inevitability and uncertainty of what was coming and what one clearly desired.

Fr. Lob looked at snow-covered city blocks from Liteiny Bridge—in childhood, he remembered, there was a river here; people sunbathed by the walls of the fortress. People sunbathed in winter too. He also used to go to school, it seemed. Of course he did. There were... strange lace curtains there and that ineradicable smell of mashed potatoes (it imperceptibly merged with the first sexual dreams—this association was later very hard to get rid of), and the school janitor kept a goldfinch in a cage. Commune with what you extracted, link up with the person you follow. Quite. It's time I did. Looking from the bridge at the artificial hill with a sugar-carved church lit by feeble colored rays, Lobov absent-mindedly (more likely out of habit) wanted to understand further how everything that surrounds him could have any relation to him. He mechanically touched his cheek with a finger; there, a recent shaving cut still called attention to itself with its narrow freshness. The feeling of the finger and the skin on his cheek for a second merged in one. A possible depth was lost in the touch. Time is destroyed in any point of utterance; the speed of its decay depends on the intention to continue. Every body part has a name that means nothing. We used to shoot pigeons with a pellet gun. In his recent conversation with a young writer in a café, he tried to speak to the same subject, but said something else, and now this something also occupied his thoughts, coming uninvited to take a place in the "surroundings" because the writer's words about the "music of language" surprisingly didn't cause the expected repulsion, but, on the contrary, reminded him of something he thought necessary to clarify—like a forgotten word sometimes makes you think that should you fail to remember it, all that you've painstakingly collected over the years would monotonously start to disappear—therefore, having possibly missed a link in the reasoning of his new acquaintance, or perhaps secretly pleased of the arising opportunity, he said that he required only one thing of music (any music). He required that music not irritate. With either its "passion", its "harmony", its volume, or its "beauty". He then said that such music satisfactory to his taste would initially appear to be the absence of any music at all—its dissolution in the noise of his hearing, in the *anticipation* of music, in other words.

I have in mind the kind of music, he thought, that develops backwards, as it were, and possibly emerges from my body combined of various sequences, directions, punctuations, and substitutions—but I don't insist on the inevitability of such a sensation. Yes... indeed, a sensation, despite the unintelligibility of the word. The delusion drifted behind me like the smoke of a fire on the steppe. We were driven around in crooked boxes of transparent crystalline metal (meanwhile, what for others proved to be an unbearable torture, requiring exceptional courage and endurance, became for me a chance to satisfy my insatiable curiosity, and one shouldn't lose sight of the fact that the problem of night dreams turning into reality appeared to me as a theoretical task exacting uncommon effort, requiring also an increase in knowledge, so to speak, and I waited to pronounce my "no" one more time, thus introducing an equation of affirmation into the hosts of visions resisting a solution in knowledge), and silver, gold, emerald moons, moons forged of bronze subterranean skins, crept behind us, following in our footsteps like the echo of non-being, sneaking at night, stops closer and closer to the fragile thresholds of hearing where transparent walls breathed, instilling in children's hearts the sweet horror of impossibility and a sleepy anticipation of infinity. I was most of all amazed by the silence of our lives.

The smoke of autumn fires in the suburbs burned the lungs when you took a deep breath; frosts gripped various plants. Graininess, sharpness, pine needles.

The moth of autumn burned away, thoughtlessly circling the candle of still ghostly December, and got resurrected in the thinning of the horizon that has cut apart the false radiance of its passage. A question in a low voice: "what would happen in the previous expression if the author wrote, 'sharply twining round the wrist'?" An answer: "burning the candle of the horizon, the ghostly passages along the ledges of thinning, clad in the false radiance of autumn, descended to the senseless resurrection of the outline of the preceding sentence." The duration of pushing down the computer key extracts the quantity of a repeating sign. This indicates the probable importance of another part of the expression, namely "the smoke of frosty fires", and so on. How to make no one die? The invention of an element number X. The discovery of the unknown in an equation of similarities. In the huge hair of earth the thin death of a star is comparable to a return of a deity to the eye.

Otherwise, why does it appear at all, and furthermore, offers itself as a subject of discourse? But I also don't understand where the necessity to "express oneself" comes from. (From this moment on we read what's written by another person—names have changed.) Because of my upbringing and adopted experience, I content myself with the meager idea that a literary expression (i.e., an expression constructed in a specific way) produces particular reactions in the perceiver. Thus, were I in possession of certain skills, I'd be able to produce in the reader presentations, emotions, images, and ideas whose pattern would, in turn, create the sense of immutability and authenticity of the lived expression at the moment it is transformed in the experience of the perceiver. But let us also touch upon such an insignificant and trivial point as the coupling of the monstrous and the beautiful—it's the engine of their interaction that ensures the value of the *sublime*. If we proceed from the assumption that any consideration of the monstrous is possible only within the perspective rigorously required by the category of the beautiful or by its supposed opposite, we'll then inescapably return to the fact that these terms refer to the expression that makes possible their "appearance" (even if it doesn't belong to me). At the same time, the expression in the promise of a semblance of order is determined by its own limits (otherwise the "surrounding world" should be viewed as one unfinished sentence within open quotation marks), and these limits bear the name of an error with the inexhaustible power to change itself and the surrounding world: a virus. The expression as an act of thought is dual from the beginning. I, for example, in many recent years had no worse experience than the moments (in the genuine, "elevated", classical sense) of contemplating the overcast rectangle of the window on which my gaze occasionally rested—such weather, as is known, is quite common in our parts; the instinctive terror before it in conjunction with the sound of the endlessly dripping, greasy kitchen tap which in that disposition was doubtlessly of the order of the beautiful is with me to this day, yet occasionally it drives me to ecstasy, and even after time has passed, I still can legitimately call it the experience of the *sublime*. No, they'll tell me, we're unable to continue this conversation—the ice-cream is melting in our hands, the windows are burning in the sunset, the minds are confused by the rustle of tree leaves and the thought of the nature of rustling as such; but above all, we can't continue the conversation because we haven't introduced an important anthropological dimension. No, we haven't introduced it. We haven't introduced it deliberately. In order to introduce it, one should at least refuse to consider man the limit of what he says about himself—in other words, an endless deviation from the axis of his self-representation. Besides, I'm not disposed to like people (in any of the generously suggested senses) because most of them lack... well, for instance, the desire to speak about everything at once, and "if we weren't saying *everything*, how would we know what qualities we have?" It's pigs that find truffles, not prophets.

I myself am of interest to myself only as a function of exclusion gone nuts; observing it (again, thanks to my education and training), I can imagine its indistinct extensions into various spheres of great duplicity whose interpenetrating streams seem immobile.

Like the glassy surface of the river that on occasion gets broken with ripples by a light wind from the hills. This wind introduces some variety into the sleepily trembling (the word is indeed most unfortunately chosen!) delusion to which one is, nonetheless, inevitably carried off when memory comes, time and again, in ever more ridiculous clothes to the same, feverishly recurring dreams. Every groan—even if barely audible—that broke from the sleeping children exhausted by the heat and the wretched roads of the country (exhausted by its own idiocy) shook the cobweb of rays weaving around us the basis for the appearance of demons, and then love spasms, like live electric cables, would run even over my own body to which I promised never to sleep in order to observe life in all its magnificent monotony. We continued to diminish in size in order to retain as much as possible from what our bodies processed into immortality (that's why we diminished, of course!) condensed in sticky, brandy-colored gum that crept from unhealing skin cuts down a chromed drain. It was reminiscent of a vaguely familiar engraving of latex collection in stuffy Amazon forests. The only exception was that his later fate was of no interest to anyone. The dissemination of low-precision technologies, of rights to birds' entrails, and of immortality, as before, remain the prerogative of the government. Of course, many years later I chanced to learn about the later fate of the elixir, but to tell you the truth, consciousness refused to believe what I heard from the man who, panting, whispered in my ear this entire story, probably unaware that what he hastily clothed in words, taking frantic, almost unnaturally greedy sips from his finger-stained glass, was shockingly preposterous. One has to admit, though, the story did put some thoughts into my head, and I allowed myself to succumb to these thoughts after I, in due time, hurriedly said goodbye to my chance acquaintance (was he really a *chance* acquaintance?), and subsequently found myself walking along the snow-covered streets of Vasilyevsky Island towards the Academy of Arts. Evening came. Warm snow was slowly falling. I tried to put the disparate parts of what I'd heard together into a single picture. The cells of space absorbed time, as though in some chemical process of letter-combination or remembrance. Sometimes I shuddered at the horrifying vividness of what appeared to my mind. Dividing space, as before, remained the only possibility of representing time. I saw Liteiny Prospect, the bridge across the dried-up river in place of which there were now blocks of mansions with tile roofs glistening in the rain, where Chopin's nocturnes were quietly playing and stained-glass windows hypnotically burned in the rays of the setting sun; I saw, as though through a magnifying glass, close-ups of slanted rain lines (like in Leo Tolstoy) and at the same time, behind the curtains of the snow slowly pouring behind my back, an old man on a bicycle, dusty whirlwinds and pumpkins rolling on the asphalt; I would then find myself in a messy apartment where jars were fixed on towering stands (they were medicine droppers, one would think), and beneath them a motionless body was stretched out with multi-colored wires connecting the head to three or more computers. One could repeat the word itself. There was an opinion that such repetition (probably owing to a Sufi practice) changed human appearance beyond recognition. I heard a metallic strum, but at the same time I was stealing along the empty corridors of a huge nocturnal building, holding in front of me a map and a pocket flashlight, peering, till my eyes hurt, in the complex, not quite comprehensible twining of solid and broken lines that had "*possible location of the pipe*" written on them in light blue. Eternal non-return is at the very heart of monetarism, the rhetoric of capital exchange and circulation. But when I reached Solovyov garden, I sat down on a cold bench, took a bottle out of my bag and half-emptied it in one gulp. The cigarette that followed the vodka completed my renewed interest in the surroundings. I threw the hood over my uncovered head and suddenly laughed—that's why Fr. Lob talked about Tantalus back then! Was it enlightenment? Hard to tell. Everything wasn't what it seemed; it was all completely different. Our habit of trying always to get down to the causes, to search for motivation, once again led us astray. It was then that I understood what until that moment had led us off; it was then that I realized how close I was to the brink of an unavoidable catastrophe.

At the next instant, noticing from the corner of my eye the movement of a shadow by a fence of the cross street, I dived into snow a split second before a weak bang. When I got up, I saw no one. A dark thawed patch showed in the spot where my cheek had touched the ground. The war was over; muscular birds were singing. Too bad we were mistaken, but it's three times as regrettable that we forgot the nature of the mistake. The stillness around us seemed an unexpected reward.

Silence protected us from excessive impressionability in our geographic movements, lengthy like a northern spring. Only a girl with a crew cut (her role during her village performances came down to declaiming a rather carelessly written monologue in the Russian style—about suffering and the resurrection of the soul in the crucible of suffering) standing in the corner where she thought it was cooler, repeated with equal intervals something like "I can't imagine there'll be a time when I become beautiful and get married!" A boy pressing to his chest a decomposed mummy of a Tibetan mouse—can't remember his name now as I can't remember what the corpse of the mouse looked like in moonlight—only once opened his dreamily closed eyelids on which obedient pictures of his visions replaced one another inconceivably fast and, getting distracted from his constant contemplation of the nature of understanding (I must say it wasn't particularly original, though in some sense it was quite curious and was indeed strangely linked to his scrupulous observation on the behavior of kites: it asserted that any action whatsoever was completely unfilled—as was, after a few deductions, any sign appeared in its emptiness the sum of all its possible, projected, *future* senses, which, theologically, allowed one to imagine in the same series the absence of God as His all-consuming intention to become Himself even if the ensuing reasoning clearly seemed weak and reminiscent of the arrow aporias...), said without a trace of reproach or challenge, "if you stick your finger in there, bitch, you'll understand how hopelessly pleasure is doomed to itself." According to the notes, it happened in early summer in the city of boomerangs and the number 11. It was the city where our childhood came to its end and where Asya, the girl dreaming of marriage in the corner, disappeared. It was rumored that the greedy and treacherous priests of return had sacrificed her to the second-rate deity of wind whose lips were glass-like and bloodless; they seemed to announce by their act that although they intended to neglect their duties, they were forced, for the sake of preserving the symmetry of the cosmos, to follow a routine that had nothing to do with the genuine spiritual impulse and true knowledge. And instead of multiplying the magnitude and magnificence of the number *eleven* in their contemplation, they had to take care of formalities, one of which was precisely the launch of a kite with a crucified virgin on it into higher spheres. And in practice, as far as I understand, they persuaded the girl that she'd be joined in matrimony with either the kite or the wind and took her high up in the air where she dissolved at sunset together with the flying apparatus. She may have drifted across the range surrounding the plateau and successfully crashed in the rocks. There was a castle on one of them. There is a painting: two persons in it—he's young, in a pince-nez; deer and shepherds in the background.

Few of us were present at the launch ceremony; at that time we, entirely consumed by our own fates, had no interest in the sacred rituals of celestial matrimony and binary calculus. We were trying to grasp the mysteries of a single dream and the possibilities of reality in its limitless worlds.

Something else is interesting, he notes: when I'm writing this, I don't see any city before me, and shadows of other correspondences, other places run across the transparent underwings of vision; experience doesn't respond to the things of these places with anything other than a light (oxidation... something like the fresh sourness of plum skin) surprise.

Meanwhile, the walkers must continue carefully treading on stones. An approach made present. Wrinkled air gets dark. Groves, it seems. A glimpse of dark groves in the distance—but stones: step ahead. Intractable particulars: no definition of a thing is possible within the limits of words *qua* finite numbers—the latter and the former (vice versa) always can be and always are different. To open a notebook, a window at night. No proof required. An open window and the smell of wet poplars. Why does it smell of melted snow? Where has there been a shift, an overlaying of one smell with another if the window's closed, and the monstrous noon ripening outside tears shadows apart like crackling silk? Ragged birds approach reason in one stroke of naming, designating them, and tracing their incomplete migrations—but they'll never coincide with themselves when the places they left fall at their feet; and (bypassing subjunctive snares) we may confidently say of these places, "here's something else our thought lacks—it may be alternately called autumn, an old coat with a moth-eaten collar, a deceived literary character stuck in a storage room, a cracked wineglass, a frame of intended presence, the secret of the strongest coffee impartially pouring down with Herculanean rustling, a handful of silica at the end of August and of your hand, aurora borealis in the incision of dawn, nausea, violence, poverty, Christmas night, all of the above, and also this: beware of smiling like it all means something to you—there you go now, live all you want, who cares," even though each word passes through these places when they smokelessly disappear at a glance, as if they never existed.

Much, much too much. Is there more down or iron? Iron or gold? Gold or dead people? Dead people or no one? How many lines of muttering slid, without a trace of non-self-identity, on dirty tables along life lines, past hollow, clay hills, mirror ways, and wine curdled in its sleep? Such is the agreement. Such are power, powerlessness, and the sleeplessness of agreement that at one stroke, with an irrepressible and ghostly power, extract profit from beating the air. Let's note that no one intended to mention him. And despite my approach—it may be judged arbitrary even now—exhaustion and subsequent consumption appear an act of marking the highest omission (...) in the cognitive process. "It's hard for me to grasp it, but how can I put it better..."

I reluctantly interrupted mother. I regretted it ever since. As you like—I'll try, I'll show you how simple it is. I replied. First, solitude, alpine air, an almost tactile sense of the world's primordial materiality, and then, is it really hard to assume that the system of signifiers inherent in a particular ideology, or, for that matter, any system substantially self-reliant in its self-replication—here I picked up a twig and, as attendant proof, started drawing with it in sand something resembling the skeleton of a fish—can't any longer be content with either positive, or negative arguments proving the possibility of its transition to a different level of complexity, and consequently, a changed speed of its data operations? Thus, the expansion of ideology, including its nucleus, mythology—in fact, its only *meaning*—loses control over the mediating machines of meaning production, finding itself in an extremely thick world of one-sided... HOW CAN I SAY IT? OUTPUT AND/OR INPUT? Here one should add that the structure of tolerance, advance, flash-like conversion of deviations and their compensation is transformed into an impeccable mechanism of insanity.

"But then it's all a nightmare!" exclaimed mother, her eyes still on my drawing.

Clearly.

"And when you grow up, will you try to explain it all to your..." she faltered from awkwardness, seemingly unable to find words appropriate for the moment. "Girlfriend? Fiancée? Promise me you will."

I didn't think it necessary to reply. My mind again focused on the mountain, black pine needles reminding me of Tien Shan fir trees on Medeo—other places, other conversations. Savoyan Alps, the papier-mâché of a three-dimensional map, an infantryman walking with a rifle, or shall we say a sack, no... not rifle, not bullet, not sack, not scissors, but foothills and a prisoner departing from his jail at the speed of a lonely, lame traveler. His azure, airless lips repeat something inarticulate, in the name of something even more inarticulate. Is this the name of a girl? A secret idea? The native land? Is it the name of the executioner who opened for him at night the doors to the garden of carpets and dancing caducei? Or is it the name of a wandering charlatan who taught walking sticks how to fly in the labyrinths of groves sweetly looming on the very edge of the art of composition? How many roses blossomed there on the first day, how many red ones sprouted on the third? There's no riddle here. Here there's only purity, absolute purity of azure lips. Find a name for me, I asked mother.

"Why? You already have one—a beautiful name—we're all so used to it now! If only you knew how many days and night your father and I spent finding it for you... We went through dozens, hundreds of albums, newspaper clippings, photographs, and old magazines until we found yours!"

I need many names, I said to her then (would I dare put it that way today?); I need as many names as I need deaths, because one death isn't enough for what I intend to accomplish.

"And besides, how were you to know that you were giving me the right name, that the future would respond to it, would become its present?"

"Giving the right name?" laughed mother. "To what? To what you were at the time? Just think: that which was 'you' could be called anything: rust, twig, draught, phone ring, apple, sequence, sleep; you were as alien to these words as you were bonded to them in blood—their every sound, every combination opened up a future you entered, leaving behind the ever-advancing present. Sometimes I suspect that at the end of their lives some people enter death having never looked back."

"And what did he say to that?" asked Fr. Lob.

Dikikh turned over the page.

"He said... nothing. It reads here 'he thought'."

"And what did he think?"

"That he turned around only to see all disappear."

"All people or all things? Sometimes it makes a big difference," said Fr. Lob.

"Will you let me finish?" I blew up finally. "I can't understand what you're trying to prove."

"You can certainly understand it to mean the opposite. The closer you look the more transparent the thing, its time, its promise, the grimace of its presence. 'The recovery of sight' is the liberation of vision from membranes, but reality is never so deep as to find in itself the power to become a dream. All this is known, but every time it's known in a different way." Then someone else speaks again.

"Don't you be so greedy!" exclaims mother with a smile. "Let's go into the house instead, my boy. It's evening—see the fog coming down from the mountains?—the wind carries the smell of snows, stars in the meadows promise no cure today, and the shouts of shepherds echo in my heart with the burning void of loss and youth."

Enough already, read this instead. Really, look, this is interesting: *"the Sheriff and the Management offer an immediate reward of $20,000 to anyone who will provide information leading to the arrest of any* *person or persons using violence against the employees of this filling station..."* All the dramas of recent times unfold in settings as immutable as Athens. This one's no exception. Only a Russian can think of such a thing. From the outside the plot seems pure and logically impeccable, but then you see it in all its staggering stupidity. The fragment is most unsuccessful and vulnerable. A man and a woman attempt to rob a gas station (it has to be one displaying the above notice), then flee from the scene, after which, according to the plan, a third participant—the name is withheld—is to turn the man in to the authorities (but in fact, it's the woman who does it—she thinks it's better that way), get the money and run. Meanwhile, the woman is to confess on local TV that she did it simply out of jealousy—they were both elsewhere at the time of the robbery, some three hundred miles away, in boundless gardens—and that now she can't sleep at night, consumed by remorse—she regrets her actions and is sorry for her innocent plotting—yet the scheme breaks down, she doesn't appear either on TV or anyplace else—that is, she's last seen with a stranger (one would imagine, the principal bearer of the intrigue) at the airport, but even that may be taken only as a hypothesis because she doesn't seem to exist—and never did—in the reality of rumors and gossip; the person seen at the airport is someone else—a dwarf running to the horizon through the immigration gates of—what's important here is the trail of undisguised references, even if the dullness of the referent may not allow us to develop the theme any further. A story of this sort, if plotted far more precisely, could become a good pretext for conversations about coincidence and about how the seamy side of the law is the law's doubtless affirmation. Who visited there drank mead and wine, and who didn't visit bought cigarettes, beer and a burrito, *gracias, señora*, put guacamole on top, sat down on the warm concrete of the porch, and listened to the harness jingles of the San-Diego-bound train and to the night walking on, arm-in-arm with demons blinded by the ocean star, generously paying seaside bushes in the small change of glassy cicadas.

My diaries and travel notes (not all in them is clear to me now) count five thousand seven hundred and eighty three pages. Four of these pages are irretrievably lost. Even when lying at times with some woman, stupid like me, I entertain myself by going over the imaginary pages (thereby doubling their existence), asking from time to time, what could possibly be written on, say, page 178? Sometimes those who stay tell me that the said page probably talks about love. I don't argue. I forgot what it means to argue. I live without letting go of the pen even in my sleep—or rather in my never going to sleep, which affects me like alcohol—last thing my stomach doesn't expel still—oh yes, we melt in each other so gently, clouds further out, images of birds, streaks of soaked honeysuckle and of rustling, bent tree branches, but occasionally a few photographs are there too—they refuse to fit into what they promise in the future, and at times sleep reminds me of boiling, gray ice someone puts on the eyelids—it's impossible to wake up, leave the cobweb garden of insomnia that became the only dimension of space, save for the movements of the hand leading the blunt, indifferent, sputtering tool on the porous, crumbly paper, clay, or acid-eaten metal of my diaries, spraying ink or some other kind of emptiness that differs in color from the page, stone, or skin on which in the even light of dawn one can read a tattooed request never to deny what was said, or when this request doesn't differ from anything at all—it's there that the roots of existence originate (but I didn't have the time to jot down that this is true only of the limits of indefinite tenses where well-off processes actually unfold) because above all, I want to make sure my vision keeps up with my hand, destined, in a carefully calculated way, to run ahead of the future event and the event's reduction to what happens in it. I must confess, I've pulled off this simple trick for over a quarter of a century. Nothing special. Easy as pie, just an old lounge number. I certainly have no reason for thinking this, but in my work on diaries (few, though, would consider it *work* strictly speaking; should anyone wish to get acquainted with a particular description of alpine passes, sinister cries of pre-dawn birds on bleak riverbanks in the fog, doomed revolts in countries no one ever heard of, burning fluxes, or studies of the human prime mover, they wouldn't find a single page about these and many other things), I must have wanted—how shall I put it more precisely?—to "get ahead" of the other or others in their conquests and appropriation of words from the very beginning, even though the very concept of "beginning" is clearly dubious and exists in the transparent quality of an allegorical figure. I'm not sure I managed to present an articulate tale of digression and its strategies. At one time they used to be magnificent. Anticipating any possible intention and following the logic of the established order, I had to strive to become *all people at once*, in order to retain everyone who became "me" (a human trap) "within me", and thus eliminate myself (sometimes I thought about simple physical self-elimination—who in his youth didn't dream of conquering every woman in the world, of winning in the absolute weight, and of attending one's own funeral?) or eliminate the limits of my own self-representation, and therefore of that which endlessly came in the discernment making up some "me." The thought that neither time (in any of its senses), nor space have any crucial part on the scales of mutual manifestation sometimes brought a note of peace. Which for those times (as well as later) was of no little significance. No money. War. Cold. Nothing to be done. Time to end this. There are letters (I mention them in the diary without, however, reproducing them in full) I still haven't managed to read. Much in them is dictated by the sense of justice. The important thing is that abandonment in such cases becomes the necessary condition for studying the physiological particulars of decomposition. The breakup of the reflection in your eye forced me to peer in your face even more intently—peer in the growing void of the face I'm full of today because I don't see it any more, and the knowledge of it binds me to nothing. The simplicity of inversion also charmed. One can imagine, for example, a reverse process—not an expansion, but a compression—theoretically just as absolute—a shrinking in which *is* is located in *nowhere*. Expansion and compression.

Diary writing was, in essence, both these things at once.

I also looked for your trace in what hasn't yet happened and probably never will. That's the first thing. The second is somewhere near. The third is always non-conceptual. The idea of the third can't be articulated. Its presence is described in relatively uncomplicated terms—it's simply there when one needs it. Guess, wrote Dikikh at the top of the page. His fingers melted on the keyboard as he walked away down Kirpichny Lane.

So long ago. Under a totally different constellation, under a different twilight of the eyelids. But of course, there it is—the incomprehensible town in a very different south, magically calmed in the cavity of vision... here the evenings of the same front gardens and dreamily rustling acacias are stopped in imprints, the nights are soaked in the ethereal resin of petunias and nocturnal tobacco, and the days see dust flying over Piatnichany into the stupefying nowhere, the same nowhere where the ruins of some estates are still standing, three, four times transformed into foul ashes, remembering neither relations, nor beginnings, nor decay, and equally unsuitable for the description of those parts. I remember it well. I'm from the South too, as it happens. As is Fr. Lob, who in those days was an insane programmer with an iron guitar and probably saw computers only in drunken dreams, or Karl who later went surfing the limits of the Matrix for the very last time, with a handful of coral beads in the mouth still smoking with the hoarfrost of liquid nitrogen, as did Yury Dyshlenko who became dead at the moment someone uttered under the low, smoke-filled vaults, "he died in Quincy, and the grammar of predestination immediately turned him into the Only Color of the Universe (it colors everything while touching nothing; it forever precedes the outline, the line, the number entering the wrangle of differentiation with the illusions of substance, like light and the impregnations of quartz discovering sparks of the surface—quite so, wise Rishi!—therefore, does an enlightened one contemplate *chi* while looking at them...?)"—how many of them are there? For how long? Why? Must one think? One must always think because "always" is unavoidably necessary, as is "think", "a second", or "the paradox of the liar"—we promptly ascended the prescribed arch, each in his hour, like wooden birds on whose backs a piece of paper with illegible instructions is pinned, and, stirring the squeaking plumage of the flippers, started moving in our blind, greedy rambling toward the blinding-white corners where, as was written in the seventh clause of the instruction, there was neither zenith, nor nadir, yet, upon eating the book, one could expect a resurrection from the ashes into which our bodily mechanisms were transformed by the friction of their pinions with the jags of light, night, the wind of solar storms, and the teeth of angels—unlike ours they weren't missing, crooked, or tobacco-stained—without, at the same time losing the outlines, necessary for any further recognition, in which we moved in the same exact way as in our blind, avid rambling, so slowly that the physical laws that govern the life of metals, acids, ghosts, and tides were losing legitimacy, and philosophers gliding on soapy axes of gravity and counteraction had ended their disputes twelve minutes early and were gloomily packing their trapezes and patched rugs, greasy from the countless touches of bare feet, back in the trunks—need I mention that the sun and moon were losing their meaning in the ceaseless combinations and separations? I remember how beautiful steel, burning-hot from its own perfection, bloodlessly entered that in which the first timid images showed (they were spots, lines, planes, and later the dimensions of time, color, and smell among which prepositions established the power of vectors, and indivisible particles of language opened the fans of intricate suppositions regarding patterns flowing in the hot wax of imagination)—this is how I acquired a pair of eyes given to me on loan, and I knew I'd have to return them in due time, but I didn't feel any pain, as if nobody had yet created it in me—as though the ability to feel pain was something like the last stroke, the finest detail of fulfillment—and this is why the skin separated so easily from the sticky, milky air in which streams of blood boiled and babbled greedily, like asthmatic gills—tens of thousands of worlds twinkling in hungry salt swarmed in the fog, each of them ready to bear the name brought to it by others. Someone claimed he had seen all the Buddhas—they supposedly cracked nuts, singing molecular songs of subterranean birds. We, on the other hand, knew neither exclamations, nor surprise—only speed and movement rigorously gathering the dust from which we consisted into the weight and space of suppositions. What's necessary for continuation? Embrace, fusion, sex, molding particulars into a whole, a few throat-breaking spasms? One body or many different ones? Sister has no third option. A bit further, there were running herds of buffalos; they flowed like lava in the voids of the world to which *presentations* were still unknown. Fish found shelter in the backwater relic of our being, but we knew neither surprise, nor possibility of a simple cry of joy when meeting an ordinary acquaintance by a corner bakery. What does this road remind me of? It reminds him of a frosty dawn leading to the train station. Then… oh yes, the school is behind us, right? Could it be that the old temporal rupture was a journey *here*, to this page, sentence, this line? And am I yet to open my eyes, as though those twenty minutes had been excluded from my life in order to teach me how to return—will I once, transmitting the tremor of the fingers from letter to letter, find myself in the street on a winter morning, two steps away from railway tracks, in the black bustle of a useless day? I'm convinced that only chains of similar moments of disappearance, of disobedience to the known and the visible, constitute the confluence of their traces, same as the confluence of perforated holes is the monosyllabic *is*.

Yet, it's precisely in the shining ruptures of my approaching implantation into subsequent thoughtless words that I recognize the southern city—who will dare stop me from talking about it—what—what else—when?—and here are someone's eyes, already a child's, in which we can read the inexplicably lofty, mercilessly empty sky, receding behind power lines and the sloping steppe, and of course the same arithmetical dust, standing, bluish and hazy, in a corner of the mirror, at its very bottom—the moldy green spots on that mirror could hold light after light had disappeared for a period of an already unintelligibly mysterious duration—there and further, round the corner, where branches of a blossoming plum tree hang down from over the fence. You always got sun-burnt. You got burnt around the mouth; at night, your lips were completely dry, and you used to say it was just a spring fever—too much light. One doesn't get enough of it in winter.

Before saying anything, she licked her lips quickly—you flitted by as a small, shiny lizard on the side of a Santa Fe highway almost half a century later—it's as if they got parched in an instant from realizing the importance and magnitude of what she was about to say in her hoarse, broken, unchildlike voice.

Nonetheless, they continue to speak within her, in her intonations and body. They thought up her cues, created her past, weaving it out of social security considerations and someone else's adjusted recollections—in the house of half-dead books, melancholy sun, visual arts, and the eternal rustling of leaves falling on bougainvillea bushes—in the coldly boiling silence (like hydrogen dioxide) only blinding doves fall apart in a marble plaint amid paper walls hung with photographs of karst gardens in Versailles and Sans Souci, under potter's crosses of Mexican roof tiles.

No, I don't think so. It wasn't too long ago, actually. Why, why are you asking me this? Didn't we know it? I said nothing, I asked nothing, I was silent—didn't move a muscle, didn't you notice? Yes, many knew it. And others? No, you only just thought of this—you said it deliberately, so that I could hear your so-called silence, which doesn't exist, or rather which didn't exist when I was asking you on the roof, and you, a moment later, imprudently and thoughtlessly exchanged the opportunity for a fruitless contemplation of burning ships that emerged on the surface and vanished in it—but why did you ask? One must begin from the beginning and from the rest. Did art really die, or was it someone's weakness? Just the way it appears to hearing and sight, when it arises from what's known to few. Fortunately, you could learn about it from street kiosks, train stations, opera theaters, bathhouses, and prisons. What were you asking? Finally, death changes the state of things in the right direction. It enters that which was thoroughly known. Increasing a line doesn't require widening the breath. In other words, an absolutely long line equals the environment that presents it—vacuum. Reality is possible. And to be more precise, a book, nothing else, was burning; its pages were losing color and memory in the light summer fire that the westerly wind brought from the islands, rising up after soundless water. Everything fit together nicely; there was no need for extra proof. Or possibly, it was simply a possibility not to end what was supposed to have an ending.

No one will tell us this, we're unknown in the night of slipping words; we're yet uninscribed in the maps of exchange between gods and inanimate objects of painted iron and pottery crumbs. You're right on this count: vision is deceptively pulled into events in order to lead empty knowledge with its news, and, like a prisoner's ball, it doesn't allow knowledge to move even a grain further than possible. Let's leave the black, shiny counting boards. Let's drop the chalk on the floor and wipe away the stearic traces of swarms on the windowpanes. It's well known that possibility is the limit of the known. For example, the limit of a thing is its *possible*, its future delimitation by other things, but where, then, would you like to move? Do you suppose you can cross the limits of movement or of the possible? (Why are you asking me this, why do you insist that I answer? Do you really want them to believe that I'm mad? And that we can't talk about this openly? It's beyond my comprehension that they really believe in a brandy pipe hidden in unspoken depths. It's easier to believe in the Holy Grail than in this pipe, or in the one that, as they say, will sound high and low on the day of Karl's rising from under his medicine droppers. You can believe in a pipe, in crushed stone, or in a pumpkin. Where do you look when you talk? Who's talking? I'm silent. War is powerless to overcome its own image. Imagine me with a mug of beer. Imagine me sitting on a chair by a brick wall at sunset, free of telephonic dreams about elementary particles, with my eyes looking up and slightly to the left, as poplar fluff ceaselessly falls into the great waters of the gutters.)

Toward that bird, barely visible in the yellow glass of spring sun—even though I don't know what I need it for in this dry wind. Foliation, the poverty of phonemes. Who knows? No one. Because it doesn't concern anyone. Because imagination is the only measure of the impossible. In an eternal belatedness. A circle is the image of any image.

And do the wet leaves on dented footpaths concern no one either? No, they don't. They concerned faces, touching them in the fall, and now they hover in the wells of glimmering. OK, whatever you say. And what about the rainbow waterfalls that came down from euonymus bushes shaken by the hand? Madness finds hope where we draw endless fear. At the other end, the perspective is closed. Branches always touch the one who is closer. What an excessively long and tiresome word! And the trunks of maple trees, and this desire for someone to want what you want? A quiet play babbles in the glass vessels of floats—it's transparent, deserted, and formatted by the bugles of noon. Then I'd like to know what forced her to become the semblance of a membrane, a trembling film transforming non-palpable waves into the material tremor of desire (stubborn and old like throat pebbles)—a blind *nothing* possessed by its history. But "nothing" appears a second later, erasing "nithing", which almost generates the line "a blind night, reflecting nothing". Thing. I don't think there's a better phrase for ending a narrative: "this is how our life went by." Not bad. How stupid... Stupid and strange. There are simple things that are horrible to pronounce, such as "give me tea", "kiss me", "it's pouring down today", "pour me some wine", "how much does it cost", "let's eat", "have you read N's book?". Mind you, snow is melting, and you can't stop it. Sometimes it seems that winter is over. This is how winter went by.

What does this "thing" mean? Now everything's on the left, where there's a cup of coffee, orange peel, an ashtray, and the photograph of the warm springs of the Bolshaya Kanava. In weightlessness, as though the noose was taken off the tired neck, and the body was left to hover in the multi-compositional space of orgasm and punishment, with its head bent, as if the creaking springs of reasoning (Valencia laces, a collector's blood drop creeping down the chest to the nipple—the gaze, in a foggy ignorance, went down after it—a fan breaking the muttering with the chalk of toy seas and grottos, seashells, and writing on rice paper in the wasting disease of a monotonous edification—things and shadows, light and curved, like the gilded arrows of revenge or the reticent forms of silences, stretched to numbness) would slow down the speed of interpreting this position, its penetrability, and above all, the faded paper of the photograph itself. The thinnest thin line crosses that which has no form. We talked about knives. Of course. What else?

It's quiet, breathing. It's shrouded in the power of the neuter gender. Possibly, once it was I. A plain at the time. You could say it was a place, a space detached from *non-me*. But as soon as you turn away from the measured and calming alternation of circumstances and causes of various consequences—vague, but in their articulation, not entirely devoid of merit—with their carefree and irrelative dynamics of becoming something else, which is usually imagined very distinctly, contrary to the meaning that slips away at the last moment—is it worth making such a step in order to allow the current, rushing from all sides, to bypass you at least for an instant? (Do you know of such a method? Narrative style? Addresses? Telephone numbers? Publication data?)—as soon as you turn away, you immediately begin to think about how magical and mesmerizing this movement was: something happening/something that happened (finding an echo and continuation in corporeality, in consciousness, and moreover, finding there a confirmation of its own non-existence in presence, like a lava of definitions endlessly flowing into each other along the stretched string of never completing disappearance, but only as a shadow of anticipation or warning performed in its slipping away—new leaves come out here every day now; every day and every night yellow, dry leaves fall off—fall and spring, interpenetrating seasons; too vivid; scales; experience) was a set of indisputable facts, and even in the relentless erasure of one by another, a wave after wave of facts carried you, it seemed, simultaneously filling and flowing through some deliberately established permeability of the body, memory, imagination, and passion, forming, in a lightning-like fashion, the pliable sequence of thought—idle, owing its existence to nothing and nobody—such is the spring of this year; such are probably years, centuries—they enveloped and simultaneously brought together the endless diversity of what is called "you" into a measure of expediency, or if you like, of meaninglessness, which again appeared in the shortest sensation of the slow, inexpressibly slow flash of relentlessly forking luminescence in which the blissful foliation of simple duration and of its unfolding in memory always began.

Quite right; no one intends to pronounce: the Future, the Present Perfect Continuous. The guess has been accepted. The existence of such tenses can't be proven.

I wasn't myself—but who was I then? A mesmerizing idea of knowledge, requiring no proof. Did I want to be the proof of myself? Nobody needs justification. Amiability is the principal character feature. "No question about it! He writes because he has nothing to say!" Exactly. In order not to stumble on the icy path of articulating one's own belonging: space, history, political system, gender, age. On Old Highway 1, rummaging through sec-ond-hand books at Janice's (an ordinary roadside thrift shop filled with clothes shedding the in-eradicable smell of chemical neatness; stale bread in plastic bags from the Mexican restaurant across the road—*one bag per family please, thank you*).

I'm in the right place indeed. The paradise you get to by chance, for free, without quite realizing where you are, because nobody asks to see your ID or tell them about your sins or virtues. The idea of a paradise as an empty highway. Where the Gan-ges is on the horizon, and the horizon is underfoot and also where it's supposed to be—for consola-tion. And they'll never understand (as if one really needed understanding!) that such moments are scattered all over the hazy, delirious roadbed, all along the old highway. New wind condition behind the window. Outside, there's a figure frozen in the micaceous heat; it's stooping, like the requirement of proof in Wittgenstein who is only a five-minute walk away from the cliff jutting up over the ocean. Garbage: a tree washed to its yellow bone, heaps of rotting fishing nets. Heaps of youth. On the Old Highway, as some song must have it, "on the old, broken highway." It can't be that no one has ever sung us a song like that. Someone must have had. Anyway, back then, on the old, forgotten highway of verification. Let's bend down, pick up an old, salt-eaten bough. As an addition. The actions of the "I" are caused by the need to move the observer's angle of vision. This is extraordinarily important for the plot. I have things to say—for example, "back then, on the old highway...," and so on. On what shore did that bamboo stem grow, filled with the silence of strict thought? The dew-moistened sleeve raised to the eyes. The sun departs for the far-away porcelain lamp (about which we know that it's molded from red clay and river silt, and that the emperors who owned it had wings); the shadows of dolphins interlace in the nervous yarn of the writing on its walls. People in cars parked along the beach access road are, of course, silent like the heart of the stem. Sponge. But thunder.

It interferes with my desire to lose balance in complete silence, to lose the proper meaning of the Subjunctive Mood, raised by the ocean, its high tide. This (that) didn't happen. At the hour of waning moon. The narrowing of the ray. History turns you to itself, it passes through itself like the poor, narrow gates of Good. Squeaking, before and after. Tomorrow I'll find the name, gender, and ending for it. The grammar of shifting. Yes, I say to myself, putting aside one book after another, you must hurry, cross the street, go up to the ocean: everything becomes much clearer there—why rummage in books, half-heartedly leafing through some? Images. Perhaps, it's all about images that are only waiting to emerge in the head and slide down to the heart in order to swaddle it with palpability in the first moment, in the second moment, and in the third moment too. According to some, the tenth moment is also possible. It plays the most important function in forming experience. As though through several rings of glass. Through the "as though". Various degrees of refraction. But the sum total is negligible. When she met Jean Paulhan, he was fifty. Is that so?

Through the half-open door Dikikh saw hands shifting books from one shelf to another; further he saw a room that looked like a part of some second-hand clothing store (the smell of dry-cleaning chemicals); air endlessly formed behind the wide window; higher up, a raven drew its circles, and in the sun-broken permanence, glass-like bodies of numbers and proportions took shape. After abundant light, the eyes had difficulty determining (division is what's left to synonymy—a fan of division) that on which attention suddenly paused—the silhouette of a man standing with an open book in his hands, looking above the page. Is the picture clear to you? But he himself is beyond presence, and his preordained name is made up of mutually hostile signs. Because "our days are a draft in houses without walls." Three chapters of the narrative continue to talk about the theft of the ice-bound coin of dreams—if you press it to the eyelids of what wanders on the borders of reality and moon, they'll immediately perspire with momentary inscriptions, narrating the future of the person who dared to take the coin in the hand and, as usual, washing off the dreams themselves, as well as the sleeper's reason. After that, his nights will become bottomless wells, while the soul and the veins on which the soul hangs in the pupils will be endlessly consumed by little creatures similar to lice, and the night will never win anyone in its lawsuit against muteness. What does the man with a book remind you of? The soul? Myopia? The need to send out letters? With no sign of light's intrusion. All this *appears* to me (probably, to others too) and, consequently, this strictly is for me in reality, although the expression "in reality" *appears* to me the most vulnerable link in the hypothesis. The desire to create disorder resounds with echoes no less arrogant than the desire to assert harmony. To a certain extent, most literature is the attempt to persuade the reader that the writer has a certain kind of knowledge. The distinctive feature of this knowledge is not the problematic nature of its categories, but the precise (given enough sophistication) alternation of questions and affirmations (which is also true of rhetoric, but affirmation there takes the form of confirmation) in creating the illusion that any presentation is unstable. The stable idea of the commonality of personal experience and of differentiated meanings is *sine qua non*. In other spheres of mental activity such procedures may have other names. But I'm interested in the kind of writing in which even questions have no meaning. In such writing, neither "negation" nor "affirmation" is significant, and their presence may be described as an auxiliary function in the open-ended situation of substitution. What appeals to me in this kind of writing? Probably it's something about which I'm "constantly guessing" but which, due to its photographic development in time, remains undisclosed, unactualized, unpresented—namely, it's the constant eluding of that which pretends to be present, the edge of disappearance (the verb of the Present, Imperfect Tense) that may be imagined as the balance point of "there is" and "there isn't", the point of their identity. The most empty finds itself in emptiness, in their interpenetration and mutual reflection. Indra's necklace. Otherwise expressed, it is the thinkable place/time in which the very act of transformation takes place: something already isn't what it was, but hasn't yet become what it's going to be. Will it be different in relation to what it was, or even is, in its being nothing? In the tightest, permanent flash of temporal rift and intransitive discernment—the flash isn't thinkable but is simply supposed, imagined, always merely anticipated, and therefore non-existent in the outside—certain things become visible. In relation to them, our nonexistence seems to acquire movement and intelligibility.

The first vision was replaced by a stable contemplation. Dikikh understood what caused it. The boy he saw in his dream the previous day, before pressing to his eyelids the coin burning with unearthly heat (nothing can be bought for it; it is, so to speak, the embodiment of *gratis* as such), said that people from "flimsy paper" have the custom of cutting their hair during the new moon, which generates the idea of understanding perfect presence as a proper name. The unpleasant dream aside—Dikikh had a headache a long time afterwards (the alcohol consumed the night before also played its part)—it was quite clear that "contemplation" can't have causes, just as any act of accepting anything at all, including the non-coincidence of consciousness with what it creates. The question what "lies" in this non-describable locus belonged to me, not to him. I held in front of me a tattered *New...*, but looking above the page, I repeated a barely meaningful phrase I once heard somewhere—"the human condition"—trying to fathom what I kept repeating without even moving my airless mouth. The combination of words seemed to hold the solution. Languor and irritability. This sometimes happens (I heard) when the solution is revealed without any requisite conditions. Not even so much in the words that form it as in the circumstances that prompt its appearance in memory.

And it made no difference to me whose property it was. Or whose property it ceased to be as it unexpectedly got dragged into the intricate game of three names, which most likely won't be resolved in anything more or less definite, but will become the reason for the emergence of a "new", vague attachment to what is destined to remain the infinitely distant point of guesswork originating neither in will nor in anticipation.

Despite heat and light, an indistinct association arose, offering clearly incorrect proportions. Not that. Not this. I was talking about something else. I'd been given significant authority.

The nocturnal, half-drunken confession of the landlady from whom I rented my north-facing room predetermined my unexpected acquaintance with Janice and her charity shop where I whiled away morning hours waiting for the school bus. This must be remembered. Forgotten. Heard from someone else. And forgotten again. Then I must return to the night in the kitchen and follow the discouraging transition to the "problems of history", "protestant ethics and feminism" (NOTES ON MARGINS) as such, behind which one hears the incomprehensibly direct and therefore false suggestion to "let the relationship develop" (we're using a hasty and awkward translation of a passage rather skillfully constructed at 4:30 AM). The confession clearly seemed to indicate a persistent distrust of its own content—including the uttering of the notorious "development"—the same ecstatic persistence that marked the story of the father's suicide (he was a self-made man) conducted in front of the wife as an act of a carefully prepared, calculated retribution for "everything"—but it was at this very moment (no matter how much I tried to remember later, I couldn't, however hard I racked my brain) that the confusion came, and it was next to impossible to understand the motives causing the eminent, wealthy brain surgeon to reach for a handgun (the type is lost, as it ought to be in fiction, although I personally think it was a .44 colt), take the barrel to his gray-haired temple, and, if one believes the continuing narrative (I, for one, believe everything in the world, that's why lies never once betrayed me, unlike other things— vision, various mathematical symbols, poetry, etc.), shoot his brains out on his wife's knees (yes, let's move closer, indeed: a rocking chair, a slowly maddening, icy wind howling in the fireplace, cartoons in the caramel window of the TV—sure, I understand everything, nothing's easier), whereas the action, having plodded past the weakest point, again gained the terrible beauty of a gothic novel filled with magnificent Louisiana sunsets in the enchanting vapors of marshlands, the infernal radiance of noon, bunches of letters smoldering in crypts, when after the first several pages, we come upon the actual resolution of the narrative, the "real" plot begins to unfold, revealing the "true" motives, various seamy sides of the characters' interest, behind which, there tower, like a paper stage set, Swiss landscapes of heights and chasms, forestalling the gullet of hell guarded by a demented postman and a lady from a chocolate shop. The reward is a brass plate in the obscenely emerald turf of Champs-Élysées, by the fire station, as you turn right. The curtain goes up with a sharp jerk.

The first name, or more precisely, the one with which a *different* game of proper names with no property begins, is Pauline Réage. It has nothing to do with the above confession. However, it depends on how you look at it. Another detail is interesting, he writes in the next letter, exactly ten years ago I first read her novel in a city one hour's flight from here. It cost me two bottles of nice wine, a horrible fight on the phone, and a disappointment in Shklovsky.

At the time of my writing this, she, by all accounts, is 89. No: eighty-nine. I want her to live. I think she owes me something. It's a vague debt, but a debt nonetheless. Yet it's unknown how she got what she must return. Does the term "tautology" describe some pattern, or process? Unnoticeably and gradually, she was refused—I already mentioned this, but I ask you to keep this circumstance in mind—the asking about her own nature, and equally the limits of the legend (the book), that is, about one of the totalizing forms that offer the world existence beyond any "picture" ...

"You see," says Turetsky, "At this point, I stop understanding anything at all."

"Don't stop, or else you'll stop understanding altogether. I agree, this place indeed seems vague, which is actually explained by the fact that it refers to a different episode. And if you want to know my opinion," continues Fr. Lob, "I wouldn't be so distressed if I were you.

"But you need something definite, don't you? You didn't just come here to talk to an old man..."

"Give me a break, you're not an old man!"

"...to complain of some vagueness, some obscurities you happened to encounter in the text. No, you obviously need something else... You'll correct me if I'm wrong, won't you?"

"What nonsense! OK... you know, I can't quite understand why he's looking for it."

"Looking for what?"

"Well, we're constantly coming across something like a shadow he's trying to catch."

"And?"

"Well, for example, he first left the country in the early '80s, didn't he? To be more precise, in early September. You'll agree that in those days traveling abroad on personal business was a very difficult—no, a completely hopeless enterprise! How did it happen then that he, being, if I'm not mistaken, a non-official person, a person of dubious loyalty, managed to leave for at least half a year? Something else is interesting. You know, I've many friends in Finland—I met them when we started our logging business in the early '90s... I asked them, and they of course asked others whether anyone happened to see him in Helsinki. Then there weren't that many Russians there, you know! Could count them on the fingers of one hand..."

"And what did your friends say?"

"No one seemed to see him there. There was no such person. You understand?"

"And where was he?"

"That's what I want to know. And then, immediately on return, a trip to Italy."

"You friends didn't see him there either, did they?"

Turetsky said nothing. He called the waitress and ordered two beers. He watched her walk away and said: "A wonderful place. Excellent! Here you always meet the people you need."

"You have a purely Russian longing for

meetings," noted Fr. Lob.

"Probably, even though I'm a Jew... Remember, in his childhood or youth, he had a friend named Karlovsky. Do you know what happened to him?"

"Can't imagine," replied Fr. Lob. "Don't know. He may have had a friend by that name. Why not? There's lots of things you can have in childhood. In my childhood, I, for example, had a goat. How much time has passed since then? Tell me, Turetsky, you found that friend mentioned in some book, didn't you? OK, we've wasted too much time as it is. Let's go back to your novel. To tell you the truth, it needs clarification in many places."

"So you agree that a lot is unclear here, and perhaps is purposefully obscured to confuse the reader?"

"Well, well..." says Fr. Lob, opening the folder, "The pseudonym you've chosen is, to put it mildly, suspicious."

"It's not a pseudonym. It's my mother's maiden name."

"OK, maybe..." Fr. Lob put on his glasses. "By the way. If I understand you correctly, this is your first book, isn't it?"

"Well, how shall I put it... I had other books— not like this one, of course... Not in this country. Outside..."

... any metaphor lies the next one. They're burning. Synesthesia is the obliviousness of any definition. Exactly the same as beyond any word there's the next word, and beyond any recollection there's nothing, except the naked structure of memory itself. Thunder is neither the essence of lightning, not its signifier. The time of hearing and the time of vision. Calling time beautiful, frightening, or "sour" (long, light, hard), one merely affirms one's helplessness before the speed of conflict between invisible substances. Vision is always just a linguistic operation, the process of description that reveals the possibility (intention) of overcoming the phantasmagoria of the space between description and language. The melancholy of language. As I understand, it took approximately ten years to create the photographs of Le Nôtre's gardens: Vaux-le-Vicomte, Versailles, Marly-le-Roi, etc. Touching commentaries on the French gardens of the absolutist period are usually accompanied by mediocre prints in the catalogs. The peak of the holiday season. If one were to believe the author of the commentary (a professor of sociology), gardens *are* the manifestation of power.

"By the same logic, Oriental carpets are a

symbol of the Asiatic mode of production," says Pasquale V., breathing down my neck.

The gardens of Hieronymus Bosch, the maniacal regularity of park labyrinths where the fulfillment of expectation gets dissolved in repetition, transgressing the rhetoric of the mirror in the extraction of symmetry from cogency. Last summer. Last summer... indeed, where were we last summer?... Of course, on the old Highway 101. Who doesn't know that place!

"How's it going? Do they write to you?" asks Pasquale, easily settling down in the present, filled with cheese and wine. There's a street behind the window. It hasn't rained for a while.

"I think they do..." A street stretched out behind the window. This was the important part.

"Sorry... By the way, I'd be much obliged if you told me some more about that mysterious pipe!"

"Pipe?"

"The brandy pipe! Land of milk and honey."

"It doesn't always flow. Sometimes it stops."

"A crisis!" he said joyfully.

"Precisely. And usually on a full moon."

No, I couldn't be mistaken: there was indeed a street behind the window, a needle on a moonlit night.

"Excellent. I like it all very much. How can I

get invited there?" The unforgettable view of the street from the window drove me crazy.

"Not a problem. Easy as pie. And who's that?" I pointed with my eyes to a thin man in a blue canvas jacket: carefully combed-back flaxen hair, glasses, piercing (optional: "tired") look at the bottom of which there were two simultaneous reflections—of the street and the exhibition hall. The lights were turned on in the latter.

"OH BOY!" Pasquale half-closed his eyes in an almost Oriental manner and sputtered a song:

"...MULTICULTURALISM AND DECONSTRUCTION ARE A NEW RAGE ON COLLEGE CAMPUSES—AND THEY ARE DESTROYING STUDENTS' ABILITY TO THINK AND VALUE. THE TWO MOVEMENTS TEACH STUDENTS THAT OBJECTIVITY IS A MYTH, AND THAT A STUDENT'S SUBJECTIVE WHIMS DETERMINE THE MEANING OF TEXTS. HERE I WILL EXPLAIN HOW PHILOSOPHERS FOR THE PAST TWO HUNDRED YEARS HAVE PAVED THE WAY FOR TODAY'S IRRATIONALISM BY SYSTEMATICALLY DIVORCING REASON FROM REALITY..."

The last words are pronounced in a passionate whisper. A sugar temple on a hill in a dried-up riverbed. Why does Pasquale in the first instance speak English, whereas at all other times he's reduced to the language prescribed by the narrative? The sugar temple is for licking words with the tongue. Oral sex.

But her name was different. It can't be licked, and it doesn't melt.

Dominique Aury: she took the pseudonym Pauline Réage, comprised of two preferences, two readings: Pauline Borghese and the name of some godforsaken village.

"They serve wine over there, Pasquale. No mode of production can produce wine—wine itself creates modes of production!"

"But not of reproduction!" he winked back.

It turns out (later) that it wasn't her real name. So what? Why don't we try the Chardonnay? The night leaned the mirror against the window. The only thing that wasn't in Midas's power. The formula of double transformation. Because her real name disappears during the war, replaced with *Dominique*—"*because when heard, it could easily be taken for either male or female...*"—and her mother's maiden name: Aury. A clear understanding of the signifier is lost in this sequence, as it glides along the spirals of a triple recognition and re-signification, "along the icy path of self-belonging". Fall as a season. Or another season, oozing from the pores of time. Sometimes it oozes as a definition of this or that stretch of history. I was writing to you, it seems; it seems as though here figures of speech acquired palpable reality. The arcades of such an endless renaming in the literal affirmation of an invulnerable connection are, in fact, her novel which she "*starts to write lying in bed on her side, pressing her legs to her chin* (the wandering of writing in its infancy), *in soft, black pencil,*" one of the known tools of a person's tender transubstantiation into something else, into the Faiyum hoarfrost of the person—a touch, a second touch, a third touch, several touches—the writing goes on with an open amazement in order, much later, to return to its oneiric gaps (swings), to those "*briefest moments of transition from reality to dream, sliding in their imperceptible fall along the lines of count, along the axes guiding their vague names, when flowers again gather around poles, and only the cruelest, purest love becomes possible, or rather, the only kind of love to which consciousness turns when it melts on the threshold of transition—moments in which symbols of borrowed compulsion are added to the childhood images of secrecy, flagellation, and chains... I don't understand it, but I know for sure that, in mysterious, incomprehensible ways, those moments have guarded me all these years.*"

I feel an overpowering confusion. The garden

is enormous. The name is closed. In a herring-bone spasm, her photograph cuts into that which is behind the eye. The stomach cramps, as though in a fit of purest, unadulterated understanding, devoid of an object. Thus, the manuscript is mailed out, in parts. We see how excited he gets. Window panes burn in the sunset. The roar of a passing train sends us back to Europe like a narcissus, leaning over mirror streams of messages. It demands: "more." A well-known phrase. How familiar everything is. The air is filled with the rotten scent of autumn forests. Duration creeps into every gesture, every momentary image, forcing movement to stop in the ghostly endlessness. But no! Not all of them. The book moves still more slowly. A bee gets suspended in the air. Until it wilts, like a fading gunshot. A daydream can't serve as the narrative of a different "reality." I'm telling you, wise Rishis: neither male, nor female, but also neither non-male, nor non-female. It exists only in one manuscript copy. You remember the rest: publication epic, search for the author, translations, Paulhan's illness and death. Gout, plague, fires.

Like a dog, like a deaf dog, curled up by his feet... Still, what was your book, madam?

"*C'était une lettre d'amour*" is as good as Chekhov's "Champagne!"

And in a completely different context (although you still might hear "who are you madam?"), "*who am I, after all, if not that very inexhaustible part of something that doesn't get named in any way, except as loss, and here has the name* eidola—*but what do you know about that land? Tell me, maybe I don't know this, but who ever traveled there and came back? How does his mouth pronounce the word* aidoneus? *What are his hands and feet doing at this moment? But this is what we call night and secrecy, its heavenly particle boiling in the foam of thoughtlessness, whose shadow, enveloping itself and me, as I endlessly walk away from it, never betrayed me in any thought, word, or deed to anyone—and this shadow finds it possible to connect to other, similar shadows disappearing in reflections—indeed, only through the Mediterranean depths of imagination, through the endless rustling of* skia, *thanks to dreams removing flesh layer after layer, thanks to dreams old as the world, as the separating knife dancing on a thread like the bite of a snake (but herein lies the mystery: how could a snake get to Nevsky Prospect? I may be confusing things, though, and it all happened in other places where there's more sun, and the sky is much higher)*," like the bus running between Encinitas and Château Roissy. Moving along the confusing line of the necklace (oxygen). We only need add: what a cautious coast.

The concurrence and intersection of systems adds to each of them the energy of their further existence, independently of the inertia and entropy to which the system's functioning is reduced—but we are completely different already; the crazy singing of the mockingbird communicates nothing about the lake that should have been leafed without the turquoise rustling in the thunderstorm of a childhood dream—or rather, we are *something* completely different, not something we could rightfully expect, not even the rustling noise in which we appear to each other—and, most importantly, to ourselves—in phone wires when that noise lags behind our voices; instead we are only the reverse of some fold where the right side was reflected on the right while knowledge incomprehensibly froze, akin to a drop that has chosen an instant in consciousness where moments—time itself—don't need to begin, and neither does the singing of a bird unnecessary for either the narrative viewing itself in an endless repetition of stories, or for me, connected to the narrative only by the curiosity with which the eye views the trembling of the next, drop-like letter before, following certain laws, it breaks free of the glass-like mass. To break free of "all water"? Of "to tell all at once." No need for justifications. I wrote about this. I think this is how it was. First, she stopped and raised her head, though there was no need for either action. She even opened her mouth and listened. The dry heat of the midday sun was unfolded like an empty scroll. The seamy side was no different from the right side. The eyes turned to the anthill. Hearing interfered. When you listen, you don't really need to see the bird, but one could also say that another silence appeared behind hearing in the silence, and everything around was the same, though the body ran a little ahead of vision, as though it changed, separating into two sides, as if made redundant and let go (to whom would it occur to think whether you have your shoes on or not?), and this bluish grass stem, as it were—suddenly alive, rushing to your ankle—but of course, it's not a stem at all. Yes, her movements, I wrote, had to be reminiscent of a fish that slips away slantwise without a trace, leaving you a complete fool. But a bit earlier the stem contracted in a ring, straightened out, and then moved forward on the sand. I'm certain that it didn't all happen so quickly, and if I had many eyes—like a dragonfly—and they all quivered in bunches, then everything would have been a hundred times slower. There was something further—something strangely oppressive in the landscape—the smell of railroad ties, the heaps of sand where one can lie down and, finally moving into the zones of black heat, watch, playing with fire, dozens of suns as they fly in from all sides. Possibly, running water, or the stillness of fire. But I don't see any possibility for explanations. One should rather speak about rhythm. It's all the same whether I wrote that or not. The necessity of an extended metaphor and the unsleeping observation of its construction as a process that aspires to the simultaneity of end and beginning. The third isn't always conceptual. The idea of the third can't be articulated. Its presence is described quite artlessly—it's there, as it were, when you need it. Two meanings. But the rhythm that moves it all is the most curious thing. Even movement is perceived as a chain of particulars, stopped and linked by inertia. The extraction of movement from immobility happens the same way. Its perception is always open, they said. I have nothing, he replied, I don't understand what you're talking about! They said, shorter, much shorter! You look and you see *this* thing here, they said to him. OK, he replies guardedly. Did this thing appear as such before you became aware (time in this case is a working category) that you know it, or was it after it coincided with possibility as such in your experience, with certain conditions of the possibility of any thing's appearance available to it? Does it mean, in addition, that you "assemble" a thing, like some Frankenstein, surprised each time to see its peaceable disposition? No, he replies, if I were you, I'd ask, continuing the simile you seem to like so much, where does the lightning flash come from, how does the first spasm of the intersected energy flow appear in which the thing I see recognizes itself in my consciousness? Fine, let's go round the corner and sit down in this wonderful place. How many familiar faces! They like us here, they trust us; they'll give us some wine, and no one will ever think of asking us about "things"!

But we see them. What? Things? Faces? Sometimes we see them as something else in our dreams. What does it mean?

It means that they're still the same; they haven't even left the orbits of their names; their outlines are beyond doubt—who, or what are they then? Is my laughter a thing? No, they reply to him, far from it! It's a *fact*. Is a thing a fact? Undoubtedly. First, I'd like to translate the word *fact* into Russian (and who wouldn't?), in order to find out where the thing-word first pronounced itself in action. But my mood won't be spoiled even if I were to learn that there was no "fact" and only light drizzle drifted through wind-swept trees, inadvertently assembling into various words, or that there really was arbitrariness in the appearance of the yet unshaped meaning that later finds a thing it can conveniently inhabit. It's all rather confusing, and besides, it's late; it gets dark early round here. Like a seashell. I finish yet again. 4 rolls of wallpaper (for three walls)—no need for it where we have a bookcase; a pipe seal (for sleeves); a bucket of blueberries; two 500-page reams of Finnish paper for memoirs. The usual stuff. Auxiliary words govern the savageness of speech. Crunch. Like the sun—it sets in the ocean precisely at 7:23 PM. Furthermore, it's all different. Much different. I'm running an hour late. Don't rush me. Excuse me; could you remind me who Freud is? Doesn't it have something to do with that museum... remember, the one we visited last summer in Madrid? No, it probably has something to do with your dream the night before Easter. Or with the inscription on the cigarette stand at the gas station by the Leucadia Blvd. exit. This is how it seems to us, at least, when Fr. Lob, Dikikh, and I get together to spend some unhurried time over wine and another attempt to tie together certain threads of the events that are of interest to us. As usual, too many suggestions. At first, things go slowly, but after the right amount of wine, a few phone calls to the ladies are made, and something like agonizing suspense sets in that doesn't necessarily need to be resolved; then a wind throws a handful of cold December rain on the window pane; the voices fade, become muffled—in other words, we, in a very ordinary way, disappear, once again leaving not a single mark. Who was here, why did they come, was it all really necessary? To whom? As usual, as always.

At what moment does one realize that one is dead? At the moment of death—and one learns this later from experience—knowledge must stop, but with it, death itself—that is, *my* knowledge of it—must too discontinue (death always shines in gold *before*, *after*, and *outside*; it shimmers in the tiny letter "*a*" in fields of sand: the speed of light always lags behind the speed of darkness). As a result, it must always remain another's event, a fact in the experience of another—light rime assembling a handful of signs into some sequence, as it flies through wind-swept trees. I must say, my gaze indeed glides over the photograph without resistance. In the morning, the viscosity of air continued the glow of the night. The redundancy of morning contrasted with the spatial limit of night. But can anyone know for a fact that, for example, another is dead or alive? If I can't be certain whether I'm alive or dead, how appropriate is it then to talk about such "states" of another? Two contemplations. Which of them is first and which is second? I mentioned things in the room to you. It's possible that this mention hasn't yet appeared in these sentences, lines, and words. I must have imagined it. In the first contemplation (let's call it that), a thing is given as a limit, an impenetrable border of the intention to comprehend (or better, "apprehend") this thing; and it is your intention, refracting from the self-appearance of the thing in its image and form that returns imperceptibly changed, because time (even in its shortest stretch) has already changed you. But nothing has changed. In order to overcome the required distance, a flying body must overcome some initial stretch that's in no way connected to the next one. All stretches are, in the end, located in the same temporal plane. The banality of this axiom never fails to fascinate. In the second contemplation, you go through the thing; you permeate it (sometimes this is exactly how it seems); you enter it but then leave it for the "next" thing, as though carried by the streams of durations (thundershowers) produced by things, with their whirlwinds standing in one place; and after a while you begin to realize—the way it happens in a nightmare—that there's no "multitude of things," that there isn't a single thing even. And it isn't particularly upsetting. The wind flings the window open and throws wet, dead ash-tree leaves on the table. For example. Why does this meaningless phrase fascinate? Does it evoke the image of autumn "in the soul"? What's the significance of an emerging—shall we say—"image of autumn"? Do we remember something definite?—a walk, goodbyes, hopes, books we've read, the anticipation of a stopped moment still lost in the future, in which a phrase about the suddenly opened window, the blast of rain, and the dead leaves will appear on the screen, extracting from itself its own rhythm? Changing that which hasn't moved an inch. With darkness to your throat. Is the significance of any tiniest event contained in the acquired knowledge of its inevitable continuation into the future and in the awareness of the principle of its inescapable extension as a) change, and b) invincible logic of preservation? Describe the amplitude of this pendulum for me. It's impossible to stop the journey, because the journey is you: you're the shifting, the passing in the stopped world. Blue, like the sun and air of Arabia. The snows of spring. On the other hand, my death is clearly "located" in the outsidedness of the pre-symbolic regions that, within me, precede some laughable "me" and are simultaneously pushed outside by my own constant effort. Thus, the smell of irises will always be bound up with the inescapable feeling of noon, stupor, heat, green leaves, and the sky flaming amidst the green (those days left a distinct feeling that solitude/thought/cut on the finger/dust on the desk/anatomic details are all one and the same). Can't be simpler. And this "outside" is the strangest, most alluring thing, because it doesn't yet/already have a place, and also because it, the absence of place, defies any spatial characteristics of the sort just mentioned—"outside" and "inside." Writing must be emptied out to the limits of rejecting any intention, including the intention of emptying out, and then its endless filling in the process of emptying will be the last, most distinct illusion. I don't want to share anything with anyone. Writing, I say to my students, as I scrutinize a hang-glider quivering over the gulf behind the red-hot window, as a process and as a sum, is devoid of space. DRAG AND DROP. How fortunate that the physical space of the white sheet gave way to the illusion of the monitor. Let's get it straight, says a girl in shorts with a sandwich in her hand, any sign appearing on the screen is the projection of other signifiers that are part of more complex systems. They make up constellations of commands that precede even the most ordinary of letters—for example, the *petit a* that's meant to be the source of all the rest. Subtraction.

She's an integral part of her own description. It's not even persistence. At the very least, it's insolence! But I don't want to participate in the march of the Danaids; I want to be an actor and at the same time a spectator, or rather, a spectator's gaze, the very act of vision that embraces me and locks within its limits both me and every action in which a return takes place as an ascent to nowhere: I'm saying, I want to be the time-penetrating moment of vision, where "action", "I", and (let it be so, right now I'm least of all concerned with the intricacies of style) the sphere of my gaze (where everything is always already included) would exist only as a possibility of the very possibility of signification (continuation, dissemination, extension) in a contemplation constantly slipping into the future—in the first contemplation, the floating seed of nothing, exhaling the blinding "*is*" in the shortest interruptions of the habitual desire of embodiment. In the second, the endless "*would*" without any completion in "*be*"—the endless subjunctive mood—is similar to a weak shadow, an almost unseen gleam, the greatness of the impossible to which nothing is similar. The woman tidies her hair; her mouth is half-open, as though she was about to continue... three dots... moist shine... I have no time... I'm leaving... to produce the last irrefutable proof of that which, despite expectations, didn't emerge in the outline of a judgment; but it apparently seems to her that the words she's about to say are irrelevant and don't merit uttering. The summer dusk in the room gets darker. A few minutes go by, then a few more, and a soundless evening falls in from the window. Descriptions of a sudden wind gust, an expectation of rain, or of insignificant conversations add nothing. They take away nothing either. The balance of the photograph. Dancing pictures. And then, erecting the buildings of memory, they were finally lost in them, becoming legends, an empty sound falling into the thinnest funnel of its fall. It was always this way. A possibility doesn't presuppose a "today" or "tomorrow". I managed to find money only once. It was simply lying on the pavement by a subway station late one night. I have to admit, we sometimes took responsibility for many things. Riding in a car, as if daydreaming. Changes in the landscape happen without any signs of the change itself. One could say: here's the landscape; it consists of this and that, and it doesn't go anywhere. There's more freedom in this constancy than in any catastrophe. The burden of responsibility in the end dissipated in smoke, but we irreversibly became that for which we, for various reasons, were made responsible—imprudence, yes; rashness, indeed; carelessness; what were you thinking—burning cars, corpses of cats on bus stops, molecular conjunctions, overheard prayers. Beautiful and enigmatic, said mother. Father smoked (he particularly enjoyed his cigarettes after late night tea) and watched, through the slightly eye-irritating smoke, a night moth beating against the ceiling. When I have nothing better to do, I try to observe objects the way father used to. At those moments I'm no one. But changes in the landscape in reality happen without showing any signs of change. The mysterious point in the eye that allows me to see everything while remaining invisible to me is part of the surrounding world, not of me. This is probably what she meant when she wrote: "you'll never find me." And further: "you're trying to catch the difference between me and you, which would allow you to distinguish yourself from not-yourself, but this difference always eludes you, and not because it doesn't exist— it probably does, I don't know—even your hidden fantasies (we're so pathetic!) are nothing but some conversations you once heard (you don't remember where); they keep pursuing you, refuse to leave your consciousness as well as what follows and precedes it, returning you to the inconceivable, elusive starting point of these conversations, the speech of countless others to whom you want to belong because you long for them—god knows why—and whom you always flee while also wanting to dissolve in them. It doesn't work that way. I'm trying to find the place where several years ago we suddenly found money, and I can't even remember how much we found and how we spent it." The sea in childhood smelled of death because of the odor of iodine and salt. SEAFOOD.

Any utterance has no reason behind it because it appears without any motivation, and more importantly, it has no future; it appears as though crossing out the usual mode of time distribution, walking next to the latter, and sometimes apart from it, but on occasion, merging with it, which creates the qualitative illusion of an intent to express oneself, the illusion of an object of expression, the objectivity of that object gradually infecting the chaotic twinkling (it clearly has its own logic) with the virus of the writer's hope that he's no accident in relation to the life of mutually reflecting signs into which he's been dragged by his own intent to change their "state"; moreover, he produces them, just as history produces him, relying on the concepts that precede his first movements of a writing animal unaware that the act of an imaginary utterance cancels his very person hoping if not for self-assertion, then at least for some indirect proof of his own presence. A cup of coffee, fog behind the window, dry grass in a plant pot on the balcony. A barely perceptible October wind stirs the grass, translating the trembling of some nameless substance into a vibration of outlines, into a twining string of snares, a burning by the temple, or a contempt for the reflection in the glass—lots of things can become haunting representations of a *beginning*, expulsion, or transition, mysterious because the moment of its change constantly abides in the present, regardless of the point or place where the narrative tirelessly begins. But the hand quickly (its speed is a purely abstract value since it would be naïve to measure it with the time spent on the completion of a drawing or the arrangement of signs (songs) in any particular order—this is why "quickly" remains a metaphor within the sufficiently thin folds of the attempt) disappears from the field of observation (a third cigarette in a row—two cups of coffee and three cigarettes in an hour—who is interested in this? Is it significant, and if it is, then what do the listed operations narrate? For example, on the roof on a stuffy white night. How did it end there? Turetsky—Dikikh. Everything's fine. No reason for concern. Do they have much in common? Do the operations narrate an uncommon concentration? Possession? Weak will? The ability to indulge in bad habits? Walking along the perimeter? Is this not where certain rituals originate that indeed bring to life necessary realities? Hitting the head against the wall in a dark hallway causes dreaminess. You're asked how you feel. An answer follows without delay. Do I manage to connect several words in a row only because I resort to magical operations—smoking cigarette after cigarette, drinking coffee? At the same time, the meanings of these gestures can be indisputably lost in a different context, where a different code is at work—a code that prescribes certain operations to the person intending to unfold this code into a language that describes those very same motivations...) as a metaphor that in no way produces additional sense but glides along the trajectory of obliqueness in order eventually to touch the word night (neither quotation marks, nor italics, nor any other highlighting in the usual syntactic sequence—impartiality/indifference is the purest manifestation of energy), extracted by vision from its intrusion into a combination of elements, even though vision, once again, plays a secondary part in relation to that which requires this word. A little later, there appears a need to spread the night, branch it out into the same kind of multiple possibilities, limitations, and transitions. A fleeting shadow on the wall—could it be night? Those mysterious, glassy, worm-like bodies uncontrollably floating through the sphere of self-contemplating vision—could they be night? Vision sees itself and observes its own defects, regardless of the objects in front/outside of it. You too I call night, because you, like many or all things, after the briefest moment of self-identity—this condescending assumption is possible as an auxiliary tool of the short-lasting allegory—became a spot, a foggy cloud on the retina, something that can't be grasped by either changing the focus, or extending the duration of the gaze—an iridescent spot, endlessly trickling down after itself beyond the horizon of the visible. But as you noted once, I resorted to various, not always similar methods of describing my feelings (only awkwardness is left now), vainly thinking that there's no other way of recreating you who disappeared—in the most common, ordinary sense—over a quarter of a century ago, when in the morning I realized how I was to finish something which I thought you started and which I continue now, slowly learning other sensations and approaches. For those curious: she left neither a note, nor a word, nor a shred of her dress on gooseberry shrubs; she didn't even knock over a cup of milk—as though she'd never been there; as though there shouldn't ever have been any thought of her presence on earth.

Turning the page and immersing myself in erring vision—or unfolding a sentence within a sentence, narrowing the field of each of them down to an imperceptible kernel of precision in the flowing sand of intentions, I'm recognizing that there's something here that could be not even you... actually, I wouldn't call it you at all for the fear of contradicting the use of this word by others. But isn't night some material formation characterized by, let's say, a certain frequency of ethereal, nameless emanations as it's drawn into specters of correlations in the course of its self-assertion—and this is partly true; the hand isn't writing, it stumbles on something, ending the rhythmical pulsation of anticipation, while the word night returns to the night which neither the hand, nor vision, nor memory, nor even you who absorbed and collected it like a bee are able to surmount in the pitiable effort of knowledge—but further, shadows overlap, and the light becomes too bright to follow the possibility of distinguishing one from the other.

If it depended on me, they wouldn't be there. "They" is the weakest position. Who are they? Whoever? What conclusion do I make? Rashness is extraordinarily exhausting. I get tired hiding nothing. Particularly if nothing is renewed. Why do some people like reading newspapers, train timetables, phone books? What's behind this? Some people write backwards... I've seen such poetry. What's the difference between reading St. Augustine and an ad page consisting of an endless enumeration? There's promise in both. Still, their hatred (they don't even know it's hatred...) arises from the fact that my life bears no traces of *their* lives. Nothing to be proud of. It's actually a vice. Or a gift. But my life really bears not a trace of hope or disappointment. Like glass. Yes, like scratching glass with a fingernail. Like parting in an autumn park, when you see your breath, and not a word is spoken. What are they talking about? What words have they chosen for this hour? Is it the end? They are other: neuter gender. Or rather, let's put it in a different sequence: others are they. This isn't bad either. But even this is wrong. Why though, he says.

Because it doesn't contain even a speck, a tiniest speck of falsehood—the defect they try to put up with, relying on what hasn't changed for thousands of years: proofs that the opposite has priority. The opposite of what? Of that which isn't true, that which is false, that which tirelessly requires proofs of its non-existence, or more precisely put, wrongness. Sexual fantasies forced me to think about something (on the face of it) absurd: I decided to imagine my life as it's imagined by a dim, relatively dark space (as always, any word stirs suspicion), filled with god knows what (but not fear, not repulsion—no memories there), spreading every night between the swoon of dream and the swoon of reality.

I saw a point, receding with a provocative sluggishness (at some moment I was even tempted to write "melting") to the imaginary line of my ability to perceive it. Nothing special was observable in that point—something of the order of *the first thing that comes to mind*, and it was receding somewhere, simulating a movement that was to give the place inescapably illusory spatiality. The point (I insist) was my life.

Did I say that there wasn't a trace? Yes, quite so. The point contained everything there was, everything there will be, and everything there is in it, including the time of its contemplation. It was rather dim and not particularly sharp. How stupid I had been when I trustingly opened up to those who tried to tell me life consists of events. And of something else. Some said man doesn't know where he came from; others insisted man is his own destiny, something like a gesture, gradually fading along the axes of some logic of destination. A point can't consist of a point or points. There could be no doubt I was observing a point. What's it for? Still, it wasn't fear. And it can be remedied. A sensation touched the back of my head, as if someone opened the window—but no one did, did they? It didn't melt. A lot of things spelled hope. Wire, for example. A free roll of steel wire I came upon in an abandoned house. I pinned on it some mysterious hopes. But it took me quite long to realize my mistake. Isn't this how we tell stories about our loved ones? I remember that a multitude of I's following each other in the string of a report blur the idea of who will appear to them.

Who taught me to dream of question marks? I have no idea. Nothing depends on me. I don't know. I'm told there's a lot of tragedy out there. I wonder what exactly is tragic and to whom. This is how, giving up various benefits, you could ascend to real heights where rarefied air gradually becomes a complete absence—of course, the easiest (and most dignified) way of dying is at an inaccessible height, on steeps, rocks, when blood runs from your ears. What does it drip into? A wash-basin, a bowl, finally the ground. What nonsense. Others understand this far better than I do. Sometimes it drives me to the verge of blind stupor—I'm talking about the moments when thought, on completing its course (its claims are ultimately reducible to non-completing attempts at grasping its own motive) in an environment where origin, to a certain extent, is missing, approaches the only consequence enclosed in the unconditional acceptance of its own wrongness. (I intentionally avoid other terms, such as "truth", "error", etc.) As a writer or as someone used to imagining himself that way, I believe that it's possible to be content with just one written entry, preserving it alone from all other entries that sprayed, in due time, the multitude of phenomena with the dust of bright unintelligibility, turning to the same dust together with them— just one phrase, "it's all wrong", I write, would be quite enough to place various vague guesses, rare epiphanies, errors—in a word, all the indeterminateness which to this day stays in my mind, were it not for the knowledge that this thought, ostensibly full of triumphant humility and meekness, will too end up something like a guise, the tight shroud of a chrysalis—in its pulsating fog vision is always ready to recognize the outline of the next *re-nunciation*. Such is the arising endlessness which expresses itself in the self-expending figure of pretended advance, much more threatening than the imagined pictures rendered significant by the shaky ground of experience or trust.

Thus, if it wasn't for the wittingly acquired indifference so necessary for the writer's trade, I wouldn't beat around the bush and leave, out of all that's said or written, only those few words which could, if just barely, raise the angle of vision, so as... to the greatest extent... has long been on my mind...

On the other hand, I hear a whispering voice of no relation or origin, the fascination of this phrase crossing all thinkable limits of simplicity comes from a few intonation patterns that produced it and then disappeared, from a pause that implies the possibility of any beginning, and from the general tone exfoliating in the rhythmical possibilities that develop the currents and powers of what you're saying. It wouldn't be out of place to imagine an uneven movement of asymmetrical durations inside a labyrinth, with their perceptibility imagined as tirelessly twinkling meanings that don't illuminate a thing.

But does the phrase "it's all wrong" signify our ordinary zeal to transgress the form shaped by the efforts to appropriate what's constantly *given* to me, to step outside the limits set by the form's own wish for articulation, inscription, extraction beyond the limits of the *action itself* woven out of the regularity of imagined causes and possible effects in the unceasing repartition of the world?

After another mental step, it's feasible to accept the obvious: the phrase currently in the focus of attention, re-appropriates, in the field of this very attention, the qualities which we with good reason attribute to everything around us; i.e., the phrase *becomes a thing* and, further, on becoming such, it, like any other thing, becomes the becoming of its own end, and when it enters into resonance with my "finiteness" it invokes in my mind and senses a totally opposite image—the image of invisibility and absolute extension. But this too is wrong.

Because—and I know it for sure—several things motivated my discussion of this phrase. Fatigue caused by a chronic lack of money, the number of cigarettes smoked since morning, bad coffee, and the relentless reminders of stupidity which, despite subtle efforts and cunning, one has to deal with just about everywhere.

And then, she says, I came to the conclusion that I want to see only my own gaze contemplating myself. This is why I needed you (as any other needs another, a "you").

But precisely this place—and I understand this perfectly well—is the most shaky link in any explanation of what I want. But in the next few days everything will be different. Of course, I say. I agree. In the next few days. They will soon come, these other days and moons. Other days, other moons, other people. There are even more people beyond these other people.

The night branches out into the same multiplicity of possibilities, limitations, and transitions.

You too I could call night, because you, like many or all things, after the briefest moment of identity with yourself or with the word night returning to the night which neither the hand, nor vision, nor memory, nor even you who absorbed, collected it like a heavy bee are able to overcome in the pitiable effort of knowledge and light, becomes too much, and this moment is too sharp to follow the possibility of distinguishing one from the other.

Different people, I'm sure they're all different people, thinks Dikikh in passing as he examines a photo in which one sees open glass doors in a small room with a table and a round glass vase with white flowers; the doors open into another, spacious, dimly lit room—let us note that the lack of light gives it the depth of verbosity—and someone with an indecisive (pensive? fixed?) expression is standing by the table with his hands propped on it, as if listening to another person who is most probably not far away, outside the frame, but what's more eye-catching are the specks of light along the ceiling, as if from the windows of cars passing down below, and the quiet, monotonous noise of the evening street—a stuffy, hot summer is almost over; usually there's no one to be found in the city at this time; grass is burning on the horizon, and if anyone calls, it spells trouble or uninvited guests (hardly a pleasant thing either); over there we have the other side of the street—coins, open windows, lace curtains, conversations blending with the street noise, and further, on the right, the Church of St. Simon and asphalt reddening with the glow of the sun. Sure, they're different people. But will it all change in the next few days? This person has one name, that one another; a few more different names are there as well. Not many, actually, but enough for now, enough to last till the next few days, and meanwhile we can use small steps to cover the distance to the local train station, counting along the way the beads of objects which exceed the speed of foot movement, rushing ahead and vanishing behind the back of the head, behind the back, in the weeds of the station plaza, in the thicket of bluish euonymus. The gesture of resistance moves the sentence still further on. I must remember at least their last conversation about loneliness, the one which required an unbearable attention to detail. One could get to the pantry from the hallway. The smell of sunflower oil lingered in it for years. Once my sister and I saw someone's tall shadow stirring in the pantry. To enter the house of blinding heat. That's what it means. There was a chomping noise coming from the shadow. A wonderful, roguish German shepherd—the dog my father trained and reared... It stood on its hind legs, propping itself with one paw on the shelf with a jar of pickled herrings, and was trying to pull out a fish with another.

Through the needle's eye of enumeration. In childhood incompleteness pleased.

But in childhood we didn't know that word. Reticulation.

The only strange thing is that I can't notice it immediately. It's the usual physical sensation of completely isolated knowledge.

Studying the structure of the page in the merciless sun, it was hard to imagine that some letter could appear on the paper.

No, I positively don't recommend looking into my reasoning. What's its nature? Where does it come from? Does it remind you of voices or of the cortical bones of some unknown musical instruments? You need to collect your thoughts—the question isn't easy.

There was only one request: not to ask questions. Yet the questions that arise form some sort of an architectural interplay.

I used to have lots of things. I only lacked the desire to have them. I reached out for a cigarette, but then I looked at her and realized that she hadn't been listening to me all this time, and her eyes, coated with some kind of moisture, were empty and bottomless like that time when we were both dissolving in the mud of a cowshed, doomed to fury and memory.

But her eyes still met my gaze. Her dry, hot

fingers touched my cheek, after which she stood up sharply, stepped over to the table and adjusted the flowers in the vase. It wasn't late. And so on. It happens to everyone. An empty Saturday night in a summer city.

I noticed that the pattern on the silk of her dress had changed slightly. I may have told her even that new lines appeared in it—perhaps some new colors or tangles. She stood silent by the hotly breathing open window and then said that everything I'd been telling her was probably true, that there wasn't a snake but an ordinary phone booth, and also a coincidence, a crowd, and besides there was heat, soft asphalt, and so on, and that it was worth thinking about it all over again because she had lots of time, and should she tell anyone how much time she had, they wouldn't believe her—actually she herself wouldn't believe it, should someone tell her about it; then she smiled and stepped over to me again—but you, she said, shouldn't give it too much thought.

"It would be good if it was a simple phone booth…"

"I'm not too clear about many things myself," she interrupted and again put both hands on my forehead. I felt them chilling quickly. No wonder, the evening was coming to an end.

"Because it's very hot, and your forehead is burning."

It may have beenthis way. But a new quality appeared in the things around me. For example, it seemed that now I could easily see through her hands.

"And what do you see?" she asked, moving aside and suddenly somehow aging before my very eyes.

I didn't answer because I knew she wouldn't care what I'd say because she apparently also wouldn't care that I couldn't see anything besides ten suns—had I started telling her about it, I would have failed because I saw ten suns slowly merging into one—neither large nor small, neither bright nor dark—and as they came closer together, disappearing in each other, I saw their light change.

They changed from ordinary green suns into burning blue, lilac, pulsating rags of the lightest flame that gradually formed a single, boiling disk—black, as if swelling with the immeasurable depth of invasion. Her ten fingers, ten suns came together in one black aperture. Which was right.

Because I felt myself leaving through this door, as though tearing a curtain of mercury, as though effortlessly adding word to word, and no one cares who will come into the world and how. Will come out. Some grammatical forms are perfect and beautiful like musical instruments. Should one let go of them even in water? Water is one part of history. Sand the other. That's why.

My eyes must have been open all this time—the eyes I once was given on loan, and now knew it was time to give back, although I understandably felt no pain, only thirst. I think so because, as I cheerfully walked past the boiling hieroglyphs of orbits, I continued (for how long?) to see in my field of vision a few remaining shadows standing over me, as if in expectation.

But there were no more suns. What else was there to expect? Of course, they may have moved over to the left or to the back. Or were covered with clouds or shadows. It didn't interest me in the slightest. I was thirsty.

That's what interested me. I'd been aware of thirst for a long time. I could only guess the meaning of "a long time", but I knew I'd been aware for a long time that I was thirsty, and licking my lips with my parched tongue, as useless as the very desire, I thought I should try to say somehow what I'd wanted to say *for so long.*

But someone's voice is ahead of me already; it doesn't let me speak; its approach and questioning are relentless. The voice is unbearable. It's as disgusting as anything made of clay, saliva, and the trembling of certain membranes. It's a pity we still haven't learned the composition of dirt.

"Karl, can you hear me?"

"Karl...," a second voice repeats a third higher.

"Karl," others join in.

(At this moment it seems that I once knew them well—voices from the good old days.)

"Did you find, at last, what you were looking for?"

"No," answers someone, as though from behind, from afar. And as though replying:

"No, I don't remember looking for anything."

Obviously.

I couldn't have answered better myself.

TRANSLATOR'S AFTERWORD

ARKADII DRAGOMOSHCHENKO IS one of the most dazzling and influential authors in contemporary Russia, but is perhaps the least appreciated among them. His is not a household name in his own country and it probably never will be. According to Gilles Deleuze, "everyone can talk about his memories, invent stories, state opinions in his language; sometimes he even acquires a beautiful style, which gives him adequate means and makes him an appreciated writer." Yet "digging under the stories, cracking open the opinions and reaching regions without memories, when the self must be destroyed" is a different matter. The means must remain inadequate, for at stake here is a "becoming-other of language": the creation of a style that pushes language to the limit, "to an outside or reverse side that consists of Visions and Auditions that no longer belong to any language." It is the *becoming-other* of language that interests Arkadii Dragomoshchenko above all else, and it is precisely for this reason that his work cannot be inscribed into any of the categories of either popular or even easily accessible high-brow literature. Reading Dragomoshchenko requires a significant learning—or rather *un*-learning—effort. One must unlearn how to read if by reading one understands an act of capturing meaning in the snares of comprehension.

Consider: "What I really need in an utterance... is to make every utterance senseless... to reduce everything said to an inarticulate residue, like an anticipation, murmur, indistinct subterranean boom..." This confession buried deep in *Chinese Sun* is perhaps a direct gloss on how this text is to be read, for it defies all normative expectations. The author calls his book a novel, but any canonical definition of that genre is hardly applicable here as none of the characters are completely individuated and are at times interchangeable. Their voices merge with the first-person monologues and digressions of the narrator whose role is just as dubious as theirs. In addition, *Chinese Sun* has neither a definite setting, nor a definite timeframe. Some of the places are often recognizable as St. Petersburg, cities in Ukraine and Southern California, but the text shifts between them just as easily as it refuses to introduce any temporal markers: "Being means relentless transition. The point of departure is as relative as dirt under fingernails, immortality, the crawling of maggots in a rotting heap, and the phosphorescence of the outline of objects that live in the burrow of consciousness." Indeed, Dragomoshchenko's novel can be read from any random page without damaging the reader's perception.

Chinese Sun seems to allow only one certainty: somehow one always knows that it is a work of memory. And yet, it is anything but a series of autobiographical narratives or even snapshots. Instead, it declares on the very first page that "remembrance is direct speech raised to the power of interminable obliqueness" and meticulously follows this principle throughout. The promise of a straightforward mnemonic narrative is at every point disrupted by poetic observations on the act of perception that is both identical with, and different from, the act of remembering. As the author explains elsewhere in the text, "Individual facts held by memory in a particular sequence or chain, remain isolated facts extracted from a certain moment of time (this may be the origin of the mysterious, vertiginous charm and elusiveness they sometimes occasion). Subsequently, something else *is becoming*: not facts themselves, not events, but the way in which they correlate with my/your current intentions, with my today's desire, intent." It is the experience of *becoming* that unfolds into the ever-expanding labyrinth at whose heart lies the gap of the indefinite, the impersonal, and the always forgotten: "It is preferable to write about something that never happened—childhood—or something that will never happen—death."

Following Proust's famous dictum, Deleuze insists that literature "opens up a kind of foreign language within language, which is neither another language nor a rediscovered patois but a becoming-other of language, a 'minorization' of this major language, a delirium that carries it off, a witch's line that escapes the dominant system." It seems that another thing is also true (Proust's translator Walter Benjamin would agree): the degree of foreignness opened up by specific works determines their appeal to translators. But then there is always the challenge. How does one translate the kind of text whose complex syntax aims for the interstices of language and sends language into delirium? It is undoubtedly the formal features of this landscape that the translator must recreate with utmost precision, for the signifier of Dragomoshchenko's prose is also quite inseparable from the signified. Being inflected, the Russian language allows strings of cases seamlessly to extend sentences, endlessly to augment and qualify nouns and verbs. Dragomoshchenko explores this capability of his language to a considerable extreme, and yet the Russian reader will hardly find his expression particularly strained or artificial: one glides across the surface of his textual landscape without much effort. The realization of impeded comprehension is then all the more unexpected and striking. Thus the task of the translator facing Dragomoshchenko's writing is to match its idiosyncratic formal effect as much as any other aspect of meaning. Yet English is far less adaptable to the endless winding of clauses and modifiers, which means that the precise syntactic structure of the original must be retained at the expense of the natural rhythms of the English sentence. I chose to try to maintain the semantic possibilities inherent in the formal complexity of the Russian text by preserving the sentence length in the translation. In order at least partially to preserve the smoothness of the original, I had to "rehash" clauses within some sentences, to accentuate certain grammatical relations, and, of course to make extensive changes to original punctuation. Similarly, certain semantic sacrifices had to be made in order to recreate striking alliterative effects. My initial intuition was to begin translating without first attempting to analyze the text at hand, without first conducting the customary job of dissection in order to isolate particular difficulties. I wanted to read the text by translating it into a foreign language. I am now quite certain that my intuition proved right: getting a feel of the text by groping in the dark led me to those little blinding flashes, like bullet holes in its its fabric. Retracing every word of the novel put me in tune with its tonality, its elusive logic and meditative rhythm. Any subsequent revisions mostly aimed to perfect the sound of those tones and rhythms in the English translation rather than to crystallize the meaning of the Russian original.

Dragomoshchenko chose a very peculiar cover illustration for the Russian edition of his book: a family snapshot taken against the sun, in defiance of the most basic rules of photographic exposure. This cleverly manipulated image stands in ironic relief to the novel as both the sun and the family are clearly visible in the cover photograph. By contrast, the sun of the text gives us only dark outlines of that which can never be seen. But the clarity of that vision is undeniable: the Russian reader faces *Chinese Sun* head on. I can only hope that so will the reader of this English version.

I wish to acknowledge all manners of support that made possible this translation. I thank the University of Canterbury in New Zealand for a generous research grant that allowed me to travel to St. Petersburg in 1999 and 2000 to work on the translation in close collaboration with the author.

As I was translating into a non-native language, expert editorial help was essential. My utmost gratitude goes to Terry Myers who agreed to polish my imperfect English and spent several weeks burning the midnight oil with the draft. His participation would not have happened without the keen involvement of Margarita Meklina. I also thank Andrea Westmerland who provided editorial assistance in the earlier stages of the project. I am grateful to Jacob Edmond for helpful advice. I thank Genya Turovskaya for her careful proofreading.

A special word of thanks is due to Matvei Yankelevich and Ugly Duckling Presse whose enthusiasm made the publication of this very non-commercial text a reality.

Finally, I thank Arkadii and Zina Dragomoshchenko for years of friendship and unwavering support.

—EVGENY PAVLOV

THE EASTERN EUROPEAN POETS SERIES from Ugly Duckling Presse has, since 2003, been dedicated to publishing the work of contemporary Eastern European poets in translation, émigré authors who write in English, and influential poets of the Eastern European avant-garde whose work is not widely available in English translation.

This book, and the series as a whole, was made possible in part by our subscribers, individual donations, and by a grant from the New York State Council on the Arts, a state agency.

www.uglyducklingpresse.org/eeps.html